THE STRANGEST Cat & Dog STORIES

Janusz Talalaj

Hill of Content
Melbourne

First published in Australia 1996
by Hill of Content Publishing Co Pty Ltd
86 Bourke Street Melbourne 3000

© Copyright J. Talalaj 1996
Cover design: Gavin Van Landenberg
Typeset by Figment, Fitzroy, Victoria
Printed by Australian Print Group, Maryborough, Victoria
National Library of Australia
Cataloguing-in-Publication data

Talalaj, Janusz Joseph.
  The Strangest Cat and Dog Stories
  ISBN 0 85572 268 1.
  1. Cats – Anecdotes. 2. Cats – Folklore. 3. Dogs – Anecdotes.
  4. Dogs – Folklore. I. Title.

636.7

Contents

Chapter One

Dogs with incredible abilities

Talking dogs

One day in 1965, a man by the name of Rudy Galluci, came to service the furnace at the home of a Mrs Genova in Torrance, California. When he saw Mrs Genova's pet dog, a chihuahua called Pepe, Rudy greeted it. To his astonishment, he heard the reply, 'Hello, how are you', spoken in a very strange high pitched voice. Rudy nearly fainted. He thought he was hearing things. And the dog added 'I love you'.

'I could feel my hair rise,' Rudy said later to a reporter from the local trade magazine *Gas News*: 'I was actually looking the dog square in the eyes. I saw his mouth open and heard the voice coming out.'

Mrs Genova confirmed to him that her dog could really talk. She also gave him permission to take the dog to his office to show to his mates.

Journalist Clare Adele Lambert spotted the article in *Gas News* and contacted Pepe's owner. Ms Lambert's description of the dog's incredible ability then appeared in *Fate* magazine: 'A little singing sound starts in Pepe's throat as his muscles begin to move. Then he lifts his head, opens his mouth wide and sings the words in a loud voice for so small an animal.'

Clare Lambert claimed that Pepe did not speak only in a monotone: 'He sings rather than talks, although really it is a combination of both. With each phrase he goes up and down the scale using three or more tones.'

The dog became famous in the US and demonstrated his skills on television a number of times. But Susy Smith, another writer, was not convinced of Pepe's speaking abilities. Although she did not actually hear him speaking, she interviewed a number of people who had heard Pepe first hand or on television. Several of them confirmed that the dog really did speak. They compared his efforts with the sounds made by a child learning to talk. Some though, asserted it was only the dog's intonation that created the impression he was talking.

Pepe was not the only dog which was claimed to be able to talk. According to Dr William Perkins of the University of Southern California's Speech Clinic, Mrs J. T. Davis of Midvale, Utah owned a dog who could say twenty words. The dog, called Mr Lucky, was a Boston terrier. Although his pronounciation of letters S and R was incorrect, the dog's words were still comprehensible. When speaking, his voice resembled the mechanical utterances of a talking doll.

Mr Lucky's incredible ability was witnessed by reporters from the Salt Lake City *Desert News* and later revealed to the world in April 1953 in an Associated Press dispatch. According to the reporters, the dog could even say simple sentences such as 'I want my Mommy', 'I want some', and 'I will' or 'I won't'.

One of the best psychics was a dog

In the early 1970s the London Daily Mail rated a Denver psychic one of the best ever prophets. This should not have surprised anyone; obviously some people can predict future events better than others. In this case, however, there was an enormous difference; the psychic was not a person, but a dog. To be precise, a Boston terrier by the name of Missie.

She was born in 1955. Even the story of her birth was unusual. The mother bitch had delivered three puppies in her litter and it appeared that no more would be born. A few hours later, though, the bitch began suffering from convulsions of pain. She was taken to hospital and operated on. Near her ribcage the vet located a tiny unit of flesh. At first it was thought to be an unwanted growth, but they then found another canine baby.

The new-born puppy never knew her canine mother nor her siblings. In fact from the early days of her life she only knew her owner, Mildred Probert who was like a human mother. As a result, Missie grew into a weird dog that never cared for other dogs. She preferred the company of *Homosapiens*. She was very tiny for a Boston terrier. She had deep cobalt blue eyes.

Missie's abilities were recognised by chance when she was nearly five years old. One day, Miss Probert and her own mother, accompanied by the dog, were walking in the street when they met a friend with her young son.

Mildred asked the boy how old he was. The boy did not answer. His mother told the two women that he was three. Mildred, however, did not give up; she wanted the boy to say 'three'. Again the child sulkily did not respond. Instead Missie barked three times. Everyone laughed. Mildred Probert then asked the dog his own age. To the women's great surprise, Missie barked four times.

To eliminate the possibility that the dog just happened to bark four times without understanding the question, Mildred asked another; how old would Missie be next week. The answer was five barks. The dog was right once again.

Encouraged by her pet's achievements, Mildred Probert began to investigate just how much she knew. She began by testing Missie with her fingers, asking the dog how many were being held up. Each time the dog provided the correct answer. Mildred made the questions more difficult, even asking the dog to add up. Once again, without exception, Missie gave correct answers.

Later, Mildred found that Missie could also subtract. The dog's other abilities included knowing telephone numbers and street numbers. For multidigit numbers, the dog would bark the appropriate number of times for the first digit, pause, then bark out the second one and so on. For zero, the dog uttered a strange muffled sound. Missie also knew how many letters were in a person's name.

She had her own peculiar way of saying yes and no. For yes, she uttered the sound 'uh-huh' and then barked three times. For no, she went 'huh-uh' and barked twice. She also shook her head for yes and no.

Soon Missie became a great attraction at parties. She could tell people how many coins they had in their purse, or how many beans were in a sack. The dog entertained people by giving dates of birth and rendering the serial numbers of banknotes.

And Missie could foresee future events. She made her first prediction on 15 October 1964. It happened like this. In a shop one day, Mildred Probert asked the assistant how many weeks it was before the presidential election. Not giving the shop assistant time to answer, the dog barked it for him: three followed by another question, 'How many days until the election?' The answer was once again correct.

The shop assistant then insisted that Mildred Probert ask who would win the election. At first, Miss Probert, refused but finally she was persuaded to do so by the others who had now gathered in the shop. She asked: 'If Mr Johnson is one and Senator Goldwater is two who will win the election?' Missie barked once. Reluctant to accept that a dog can predict the future, Miss Probert twisted the question around: 'If Barry Goldwater is one and Lyndon Johnson is two, who will win the election?' Missie barked twice.

Her forecast became widely known because one of the onlookers rang the *Rocky Mountain News* with the story.

That was not the only significant event Missie predicted accurately. Some of the dog's other correct predictions were:

1. Nixon eventually winning the presidency.
2. Outcome of many state and national elections although some appeared highly unlikely at the time.
3. The delays in the launching of Gemini 12, space probes and moon landings.
4. UFO sightings.
5. On New Year's Eve 1966, on the radio, Missie correctly forecast scores for forthcoming football games and World Series baseball.
6. In many cases the dog predicted correctly the date, sex and weight of an unborn child.

Missie even predicted her own death, which came when she choked to death in May 1966. According to Mildred Probert, on that day, she kept barking the time eight o'clock. When asked what the time was, she barked the correct time followed immediately by barking eight o'clock. She barked eight o'clock seven times that day. Missie died at exactly eight o'clock. Later Mildred found Missie's toy clock which had been turned to eight o'clock.

Canine polyglot

Sam van Arsdale of Sedalia, Missouri owned a black-and-white Llewellyn setter called Jim. One day, when Jim was three years old van Arsdale as a joke told his dog to point out an elm tree. To his indescribable surprise, Jim promptly went to the nearest elm and placed his paw on the trunk. Convinced that the dog's reaction must have been a coincidence Sam asked him to point out a different species of tree. Once again the dog succeeded.

Gradually, the news of the canine genius began to spread. Eventually it reached scholars of the University of Missouri School of Education. They decided to examine the abilities of this unusual dog.

The researchers went to Sedalia, monitored the dog and confirmed that the incredible stories about his abilities were true.

The scientists also discovered that Jim could accomplish the same feat in other languages as well. He could point out a specific licence plate, when asked in French. Jim answered correctly when asked in German to indicate a lady dressed in blue, or to show a person with a specific feature.

In fact the dog never made a mistake. But the researchers rejected the possibility Jim could understand foreign languages. They insisted that the explanation was that Jim communicated with his master through extrasensory perception.

Dog who could play the piano

According to the Denver *Post*, Mrs C. K. Wilderson of North Denver, owned a dog that could play the piano. The dog called Tramp sat at the piano and played by hitting the keyboard with both his paws. The dog-musician kept time with his tail and 'sang' a yowling song to the accompaniment of his own piano music.

Canine typist

Alan MacElwaire, a reporter from the London *Sunday Times* told of a dog which appeared to have fully mastered the keyboard of a typewriter. The dog, named Arli, was an English setter. He belonged to Mrs Elizabeth Mann Borgese, the daughter of the Nobel Prize-winning writer Thomas Mann.

Arli began to use the typewriter effectively when he was six years old. He was able to type words of up to four letters, using his nose to press the keys. Mrs Borgese spent a great deal of time teaching her pet this incredible skill. The first words he typed were 'dog' and 'cat'. After more work, he was able to type such simple statements as 'go to bed' and 'bad dog'.

Dog who married people

There seemed nothing unusual about Kath and Vernon Dilurs being married in March 1989 at Saarbrucken in Germany. But the very bizarre ceremony was performed by Kath's Alsatian dog named Jules.

He had been ordained by mail-order ministry. Jules is said to be the first-ever canine curate. He is entitled to perform marriage ceremonies.

Best mother in the world

The best mother in the world was a female dog named Kali. She could be called a supermum. But she never had a litter of her own. Kali was not given the opportunity to bear puppies; instead her babies belonged to four different species of animals. No human mother could ever compete with her.

Kali's career as a supermum began in 1978 when two ten-day old lion cubs arrived in a pet park where she lived. When Kali saw the little orphans her nipples began to swell with milk and she became a perfect mother to the cubs. Kali suckled the lion cubs until they were ready for solids.

This first incredible success was repeated when two small pumas lost their mother. Kali later also became the proud mother to a pair of Arctic foxes and, finally, of a baby leopard. Her milk began to flow each time she saw an abandoned baby animal.

Kali was a mixture of Labrador, collie, Alsatian and a few other breeds too. She lived at Guilsborough Grange bird and pet park near Northampton in the United Kingdom.

Scientists prove dogs' telepathic ability

In the early 1970s, an experiment to demonstrate the telepathic ability of dogs was performed at Rockland State Hospital in Orangeburg, New Jersey, USA. Two rooms were built; they were vibration-proof and sound-proof. Two hunting beagles were locked in one of the rooms and could be observed through a hidden panel. In the second room pictures of wild animals were projected on a screen. The dogs' owner shot an airgun at the pictures. Each time he fired at a slide, the dogs in the other room showed signs of wild excitement, despite the fact that the rooms were sound- and vibration-proof. That the dogs could perceive their owner's actions can only be explained as telepathic ability.

In another experiment, a bitch was placed in one room and her puppy in another. Again, the rooms were sound- and vibration-proof. Both animals had been trained to move away with fear when a rolled paper was raised at them in a threatening manner. Then, when the puppy was threatened in the experiment, the mother in the other isolated room who should have been unaware of what was going on, cowered in the same way as her puppy.

In a third experiment, the female owner of a boxer dog was asked to stay in one room. Her pet was placed in the second with an electrocardiograph attached to its body to register reactions. The woman was not informed about the intent of the experiment. While she was sitting quietly in her room, a stranger suddenly entered, and started shouting abuse at her and threatening her with physical violence. As soon as the man began abusing the woman, the dog's heartbeat raised significantly. The woman admitted later that she had been genuinely scared.

Dr Aristide Esser, the project director, concluded that some dogs must have telepathic ability. In a press interview he stated: 'There is no doubt in my mind that some dogs, particularly those with a close relationship with the owners, have highly developed ESP . . . the power is so strong that I'm sure it could hold the key to understanding ESP'.

First scientific evidence of man–dog long distance communication was provided when a team of researchers from the Austrian television network ORF recorded the phenomenon on film.

Under closely controlled conditions, the TV team investigated the abilities of Jaytee, a five-year-old terrier cross belonging to Miss Pam Smart from Ramsbottom in Lancashire, England. Miss Smart had claimed that her dog knew when she was on her way home. At that moment Jaytee always perked up and went over to sit by the window.

Two television crews were involved in the test. The first team followed Miss Smart with the camera, while she walked around the village, about half a kilometre distant from home. The second team watched the dog. After a few hours, it was decided that Pam would return home. At that precise moment, as the other TV crew watched, the dog got up and walked to the window and sat waiting for her owner's return.

Dr Heinz Leger, who organised the test, explains, 'The moment of Miss Smart's return was chosen at random. The TV crew who remained at her home had no idea when the decision to return was made. There was no contact at all between the two teams.'

Hundreds of reports from dog owners support the claim that dogs communicate with their owners over great distances.

Sgt Bill Johnson was about to return home from Vietnam but did not tell his family about the exact day of his return, because he wanted to surprise them. His dog, Nellie, spoiled his surprise; somehow she received the message a day before his arrival. Full of joy she ran around the house collecting Bill's personal items and dragged them into the living room. Finally, she positioned herself at the front door and refused to leave the spot until her owner arrived home at last.

A similar phenomenon which occurred in 1905, was reported by Baron Joseph de Kronhelm. His friend was transferred to China to fight there and he had to leave his dog with the Baron. About three months later, the dog suddenly began to howl in a truly horrifying way. Nothing could calm the dog and he refused food for several days.

A week later, the Baron received the news from China that his friend had died in battle. It had happened at exactly the time that the dog began to howl.

During World War II in Tunis, a mongrel named Flak was ground mascot of the crew of a bomber. The dog was very attached to the friendly airmen and always came on to the airfield just before 'his' crew's plane returned from its mission.

One day the dog came to the airfield and started howling with despair.

The dog knew long before anyone else, that his crew had just been shot down over Italy.

Canine whiz

Scientists claim that dogs' ability to count is really only their ability to perceive unconscious signs from their owner.

In some cases, however, this view cannot be true. A Welsh shepherd owned a dog who could count sheep. One day, to check the dog's skill, he told him to run into a field and count the sheep, knowing beforehand that there would be twenty-five.

When the dog returned the farmer began to count: 'one'. The dog barked. 'Two' the dog barked again. And so on. But when the farmer reached twenty-five, the dog did not bark.

The shepherd repeated twenty-five several times. But the dog remained silent. Perplexed by the dog's unexpected lapse, the farmer went into the field to check. To his surprise he found that there were indeed only twenty-four sheep. One was missing.

Dogs predict tragic events

In November 1972, as a hurricane swept through a village in Germany, a widow decided to leave the shelter of her house to feed her chickens. No sooner had she opened the door and walked a few yards, than her St Bernard rushed after her, barking as if to warn her of danger.

The woman refused to listen to the dog's warning. But he did not give up. He grabbed the hem of her coat in his teeth and dragged her back to the house, just as tiles and masonry ripped from the roof by the 150 km/h wind crashed to the spot where she would have been standing.

The news of this event spread quickly; the canine hero was rewarded with West Germany's highest valour award for dogs, a gold medal from the Animal Rescue Society.

In another case, the life of a woman called Welcome Lewis was saved by her boxer dog. As Mrs Lewis travelled by car with her dog from San Francisco to Los Angeles, she was surprised when the normally obedient animal refused to get out of the car for a walk at Lafayette Park. The dog refused to leave the car, and his general demeanour was really queer. He barked and seemed very alarmed, as if danger was looming. Perplexed, Mrs Lewis eventually drove away. When they reached their hotel, the dog seemed normal again and eagerly left the car. Next day as Welcome Lewis was passing Lafayette Park, she was shocked to see that a tree had fallen on a car precisely where she had parked the day before. The tree had fallen only minutes after she left.

Sometimes, though, a prophetic dog is unable to save his master despite his best efforts.

The most famous case involved a plane crash in which British aviation minister, Lord Thompson, lost his life. The minister owned a small terrier. He was so devoted to his pet that the dog always accompanied him on his travels, even on planes.

One day, before the trip with his master, the dog became very anxious and nervous. He refused to eat. He began barking and wailing.

Just before departure, the dog refused to board the plane, and then hid so well at the airport that for a long time he could not be found.

So Lord Thompson decided to fly alone. The decision to ignore his pet's example cost him his life; the plane crashed soon after takeoff, killing all on board.

Dogs sense earthquakes

Scientists now acknowledge that many dogs can predict earthquakes. When an earthquake is imminent, some dogs become intensely alarmed, panting and whimpering and running around.

About half the stray dogs in the locality flee, hours before an earthquake. Companion dogs, on the other hand try to warn their owners but never flee themselves. They remain loyal to their human pack.

In Tashkent, during the severe earthquake of 1966, a dog belonging to a Russian woman hauled her out of her house minutes before the quake destroyed the house completely.

It is still not clear how dogs predict earthquakes. Some scientists believe that dogs respond to the significant increase in static electricity that precedes earthquakes.

Canine judge

A remarkable story is told by the owners of two dogs in Petersfield in Hampshire, UK. One dog was a small West Highland terrier, the other was a mongrel. The mongrel visited the terrier daily, until, once, the terrier went with his owner for a three-week holiday in Devon.

During the terrier's time in Devon he was attacked by an Alsatian and needed several stitches.

When the terrier returned home to Hampshire, his friend seemed distressed by the wound. Next morning the mongrel had vanished. But the terrier looked quite unconcerned.

Two weeks later the mongrel returned home exhausted and with a torn ear. He was warmly welcomed by his friend. The owners soon found out that the mongrel had gone the hundred miles to Devon where he attacked the guilty Alsatian and bit it.

The clever dog travelled a hundred miles each way to a place he had never been. And the episode involved detailed passing of information from one dog to another.

Mind-reading dog

Alexander Pope was a great English poet. As a child he was struck by a devastating illness which left him deformed. He was very short, just four feet six inches and suffered from frequent headaches. He was hypersensitive and extremely irritable most of his life. He had many enemies because of his strongly critical reviews of certain authors, and his political satire. As he was lame he could not defend himself.

But Pope was not afraid of anyone; he owned a Great Dane called Bounce. Bounce was a loving pet to Pope. But, when necessary he was ferocious towards others.

Nevertheless, he never caused Pope any serious trouble; he obeyed his commands and had a kind attitude towards

Pope's servants. This all changed, though, when Pope hired a new valet. To Pope, the new man seemed to be an excellent choice. The dog, however, for some seemingly illogical reason profoundly hated the man. All efforts by the new valet to establish friendly relations with the dog failed.

Bounce continually flew at him in a wild rage. When Pope intervened by scolding and hitting his pet, the dog gave up, albeit reluctantly. The dog began obeying Pope's commands in the presence of the new valet, but only when his master was awake.

The valet's duty each evening was to prepare his master for bed and draw the curtains. When the valet entered the room of a morning the poet was still asleep and there was a danger that one day the touchy dog might cause the valet serious harm. Reluctantly, Pope decided to leave the dog in the yard all night.

The very first night Bounce was left outside, Pope was awakened by a queer sound in his room. Through the curtains in the faint moonlight he saw a figure holding a knife moving slowly towards his bed. Pope knew that he could not defend himself. He was unarmed. He was a cripple and his dog was outside. The only hope was to wake the valet sleeping in the anteroom.

Pope yelled for help as loudly as he could. Suddenly, to his surprise, the window smashed open. Through the shattered glass leaped his dog. In an instant Bounce was plunging at the intruder's throat. Soon the servants rushed in and the dog was dragged off the intruder who was quickly tied up.

Only then, after the room was lit did they recognise that the criminal was none other than the trusted new valet.

It was believed that the man had been hired by the poet's political enemies and victims of his satires to murder him. Somehow, the instant he saw the new valet, the dog knew his true intentions. Bounce had even attempted to tell his master.

Great canine communicator

Tundra, a Samoyed bitch knew more than 200 voice commands and seventy hand signs. The dog's talent was successfully utilised by the US film industry. She began her career in a TV series, and her performance must have been highly regarded for she later 'signed up' for the series *Love Boat*. In 1989 Tundra was earning $1000 a day, and had the lifestyle of a great star, being driven about in a studio limousine and dining in the best restaurants.

Super dog star of old cinema

The most famous canine actor of the old cinema was no doubt the immortal Rin Tin Tin. While still a puppy, Rin Tin Tin had been found during World War I in an abandoned German dug-out in France by Corporal Lee Duncan.

This famous dog was usually shown in movies as a brave rescuer of humans. Cinemagoers saw him leaping through windows, through fire, or climbing seven-metre high walls. He saved people's lives in a flash of fur and teeth.

The corporal who saved the life of the tiny puppy was very proud of him. Lee Duncan claimed he had never trained the clever pet. He asserted that all he had done was to establish such a close relationship with Rin Tin Tin that he could teach him almost anything. Lee never lost his temper with the dog and never hit him. In fact the dog was so intelligent that he often knew what Lee wanted before his owner said a word.

Rin Tin Tin was a typical actor though. As soon as filming was over he used to be ready to bite the star, who moments before he had been tender and affectionate to.

The dog became a superb performer. He had his own private staff including a driver, a chef and a valet. He had a personal limousine too.

Huggable hero

A poor orphan from the Burbank Animal Shelter became one of the greatest US canine stars. That is where Benji originally came from. His show business career began in the TV series *Petticoat Junction*. Later, his first movie netted profits of $45 million. It broke box office records in far away countries such as Australia, Japan and Venezuela. Benji was called the United States' 'Most Huggable Hero' and the 'Laurence Olivier' of the dog world.

A famous producer said: 'Of course we had Rin Tin Tin and Lassie, but really they were no more than props. In Benji's film it is the dog that acts; his co-stars are the props.'

After Benji retired he was succeeded by his son, Benji 2. He was an even better actor than his father. Benji 2 movies *For the Love of Benji* and *Oh Heavenly Dog* were great money earners.

Benji 2 was a great actor and a distinguished traveller. He visited dozens of countries to meet his 'followers'.

After Lassie, Benji 2 was the second animal to be installed in the American Humane Society's Animal Actors' Hall of Fame. Benji 2 was twice awarded the American Guild of Variety Artists' Georgie Award as top animal entertainer. He was even rated one of the ten most popular performers in the US.

Dogs that shed tears

The strangest breed of dogs is called the Mexican hairless dog (Xoloitzcuintli). Other dogs perspire through the tongue or paws but this breed perspires through the pores of its skin. It is the only breed of dog which sheds tears like a human when unhappy. This dog also has the highest body temperature of all the breeds (40°C). This characteristic was taken advantage of by Indians in cold weather. They kept the dogs in their beds as a hotwater bottle.. Although a Mexican hairless dog can eat meat, its normal diet is fruit and vegetables.

Dogs that blush

The Pharaoh hound is the only breed that blushes. It does so whenever it is excited or happy. Its nose and ears change colour to a rosy red.

Homing champions

Some dogs have an incredible ability to cover a distance of hundreds of kilometres in order to return to their old home. If a dog is lost on holiday or the family move away to a new address, dogs seem to be capable of epic journeys.

Champions in this field were found in the USA and in Australia. Jimpa, a Labrador/boxer cross became the most famous Australian dog in 1979.

Warren Dumeshey took Jimpa from his old home in Pimpinio, Victoria to a farm at Nyabing, south of Perth, Western Australia. A neighbour there hated the dog and began throwing stones at him. So the dog decided to go back to his old home.

He walked 3200 km across the continent mostly through inhospitable, almost uninhabited terrain. The journey took him 14 months.

The first great homing champion in the United States was recorded in 1923. He covered the same great distance of 3200 km as the famous Australian dog did later, but much faster; in only six months. The US dog was a rough collie called Bobbie. His owners lost him while on holiday in Walcroft, Indiana. The dog's home was in Silverton, Oregon. Bobbie travelled back to his home through the states of Illinois, Iowa, Nebraska and Colorado, crossed the Rocky Mountains at the height of winter and trekked through Wyoming and Idaho.

Bobbie's itinerary was later partly reconstructed by people who helped him with food and accommodation en route.

In 1979 a German Shepherd called Nick was stolen while on a camping holiday with his owners in Arizona. Nick escaped his captors and walked across the Arizona Desert, and the Grand Canyon, reaching his owners' home in Washington State about four months after his disappearance.

Mystery Mex mutt

In 1914, Mexican Government troops captured Pedro Amaro, a soldier in the rebel army of Pancho Villa. He was condemned to life imprisonment.

Despite the verdict Amaro's relatives and friends thought he had been lucky not to be sentenced to death. There was still the chance that one day he would be free.

One day, Pedro's sister took Amigo, Pedro's pet dog, with her. After that, the faithful dog visited his master every night. He sat outside the prison below Pedro's cell window, waiting for his master to look out. Every night Pedro went to the window and called out to Amigo.

One night, after months of these visits, the dog arrived, but his master did not call him. The dog waited in vain all night. The following two nights there was still no sign of his master.

Soon, Pedro's sister was informed that her brother had been murdered by six fellow inmates who hated Pancho Villa. At trial, the men admitted their guilt and the verdict was punishment by hanging of all six.

The day after the trial came a new turn of events. Pedro's dog Amigo, who ceased to visit the prison after his master's murder resumed his daily visits. He sat under his master's old window each night and howled for about an hour only stopping at exactly midnight, the precise time that Pedro had been murdered.

Soon, an even stranger event took place. Amigo came to the prison at exactly the time the first of his master's murderers was to be hanged. The dog came to the prison six times, in the afternoon, at the time of each of the executions. And he continued to visit the prison every night. After the murderers of his master had all hanged, Amigo ceased his visits to the prison for ever.

Tracking champions

The best tracking breed is the bloodhound. It is said that these dogs have an olfactory ability three million times more powerful than that of humans.

The finest tracking bloodhound was Nick Carter, born in 1899. He was owned and trained by the head of police in Lexington, Kentucky, USA. This dog was said to have tracked and found 650 criminals. For 25 years Nick also had the record for finding the 'coldest' trail. He once tracked down an arsonist after the scent was 105 hours old. The arsonist burnt down a house and the trail led Nick 1.5 km to his hideout.

Nick Carter also set up the record for the shortest trail. A mentally-ill woman tied up her three children with the intention of killing them with an axe. A neighbour found them before the executions, but the children were too scared to accuse their mother. Clever Nick sniffed the ropes with which the woman had tied up her children and led police to her. She was later committed to a mental hospital.

In 1954, three bloodhounds set a new world record by tracking down a family after the trail had been cold for 322 hours. The family were lost while hunting deer in the dense forests of Western Oregon. Unfortunately the dogs found them too late. They had all died of exposure.

Champion drug sniffer

The best drug-sniffing dog in the world was a golden terrier called Trap. He was able to detect sixteen kinds of drugs as well as eleven types of explosives. On his first assignment Trap revealed more than a ton of hashish, worth $2 million.

Trap began his important job as a sniffing dog in 1973 when he was only four years old. By the time he was 9 years old, he had sniffed out $63 million worth of drugs.

Search warrant in a dog's name

In March 1976, a circuit judge issued the first search warrant in the world in a dog's name. He decided to do so in order that the dog could check out a building where drugs had previously been detected. As a result, police found a huge hoard of hidden hashish in the house and arrested the owner.

Fastest on four paws

Ballyregan Bob was the fastest greyhound in the world. In fact no other dog has ever run faster. He could cover nearly a kilometre in under 40 seconds. This remarkable dog stood 67 cm and weighed 32 kg.

Ballyregan Bob won 31 successive races. He was owned by Cliff Kevern, who twice refused to sell him for the incredible price of $200,000. This canine sportsman was guarded by two security men day and night. His kennel block door was equipped with burglar alarms. To confuse would-be robbers there were no name plates or numbers on the kennels. To further reduce the possibility of robbery, routes to the race as well as cars used for the dog's transport were often changed.

Even after Bob's racing career had ended in 1987, his owner still received a good income. The famous dog became a stud, earning $1000 each time he covered a bitch. He covered two bitches a week and performed this new role for six years after his retirement from racing.

During an interview Bob Curtis, the dog's trainer, revealed the following to the *Evening Standard:* 'I'd break my heart to lose touch completely. Bob's like a kid to me I never had children. He knows me and I talk to him. People think I'm bloody patty like.'

Hearing aid dog

In 1982 the group, Hearing Dogs for the Deaf (HDFD), was established in the UK to raise funds for a hearing aid dog training centre. The centre was established as Lewknor, in Oxfordshire.

The dog 'students' were all unwanted animals from animal rescue centres; the smartest hearing aid dogs were found to be out-and-out mongrels.

A candidate for a hearing aid dog must have special character; he (or she) should be friendly, good-tempered, intelligent, alert and must be inquisitive. An inquisitive dog will be inclined to investigate sounds, and an intelligent dog is quickly able to establish the relevance of such sounds to the dog's owner.

During their intensive training each hearing aid dog is taught what to do about a wide range of everyday sounds. These include alarm clocks, telephone and door bells, whistling kettles and crying babies. Trainers found that the best hearing aid dogs taught themselves how to react to other less common sounds as well, particularly sounds which could be dangerous for their owner.

Dog paddler **extraordinaire**

Rugby coach Robert Williamson and his family were sailing from the North to the South island of New Zealand when suddenly, a storm broke. In the chaos of waves and winds, the children's pet rottweiler was flung overboard.

The day before, the dog had given birth to eight pups, and she was still weak from that. After searching for several hours and still unable to find her, the family reluctantly concluded that the dog had drowned.

Ten days later, their dog was found by a group of fishermen on a small deserted island about 13 km from the spot where she had fallen overboard. The dog's fat glands, which were enlarged by the recent birth, probably helped the animal to survive by keeping her warm during her marathon swim.

Canine partner on the job

One day in 1989 an English army officer was crossing a bridge in Paris, every now and then glancing down proudly at his shiny new, spotlessly clean shoes. Suddenly a black poodle rushed up to him and wiped its muddy forelegs on the shoes. The officer was livid, but at the far end of the bridge he spotted a shoeblack who naturally was happy to clean the dirty shoes.

Two days later the same officer was crossing the same bridge. The same dog rushed up, and made his shoes dirty again. The victim had no choice but to ask the same shoeblack to clean his shoes again. But he began to suspect something was fishy.

He watched the dog for a while, and soon noticed him repeating his mischievous act. He dabbed his muddy front paws on nearly every passer-by crossing the bridge.

It turned out that the clever dog was the pet of the shoeblack who had trained his canine partner so well that he had increased his income ten times higher.

Dog with the heart of a lion

Cherry Kearton, the famous big game photographer of the 1920s, bought a small fox terrier from the Battersea Dogs' Home. She named the dog Pip. Cherry took Pip on an expedition to East Africa to photograph lions in the wild.

Soon after Kearton arrived in East Africa she received news that two man-eating lions had been seen near a remote village. She set off with an expedition to photograph the lions. The team included eleven Masai warriors and four Somali scouts on horseback.

They soon reached the plains where the dangerous beasts

were prowling. The lions scented the presence of humans and attacked. The Masai warriors fought off the lions with their long spears, but were unable to get close enough to kill them.

Suddenly, one of the lions fled, while the other hid in grass nearby. Kearton ordered her pet to search for the missing animal. Not showing any signs of fear, the tiny dog immediately ran into the long grass and soon disappeared. For a short time there was no sign of the dog. There were a few minutes of ominous silence. Soon though, the peace was broken by a terrible roar which suddenly broke off. Kearton waited for a while and then went in to see what had happened. To her amazement, she found the lion lying dead with the dog still hanging tightly on to its tail.

Pip had sunk her teeth into the lion's tail long enough and hard enough to give one of the Masai warriors time to get to the deadly beast and thrust his spear through its heart.

The Masai were so impressed by Pip's achievement that they called her 'simba' which means 'lion' in Swahili.

Dog with a tree climbing permit

In California, a German shepherd/Siberian husky cross called Jenny was the only dog in the world to be granted a 'Tree Climbing Permit'. Her owner Jerry Gerbracht bought the dog in 1974 at a street market in Sausalito near San Francisco. He discovered her unusual climbing ability a year later in Golden Gate Park. There, Jenny disturbed a squirrel which she started to chase. Eventually the squirrel ran up a tree. Jenny did not give up though. To the surprise of her owner she took a running jump at the trunk, somehow managing to grip the tree. Jenny then chased the squirrel from branch to branch reaching as far as 12 m above the ground.

After that, the dog enjoyed climbing trees, even when there were no squirrels to chase. But one day she was caught in the act by a park patrolman. He warned Jerry Gerbracht; trees are only for tree-dwellers. Next time, Jerry would be taken to court if his dog's criminal behaviour continued.

Jerry was convinced the dog had the right to enjoy practising her unusual skill and went to the San Francisco Parks and Recreation Department to plead for an exception to the rules. Fortunately, the Assistant Park Superintendent was an understanding man, and a dog fan himself. So he issued to Jenny the world's first known Tree Climbing Permit.

Later the dog beat her own record by climbing a tree in the park to a height of 15 m. As well, she could leap over 1.2 – 1.8 m high cars.

Jenny eventually had a litter of eight puppies fathered by another German Shepherd/Siberian husky cross. Maybe not so surprisingly, they all are able to climb trees.

Chapter Two

Dogs as doctors

Doggy kiss of life

In 1983, a chihuahua called Percy was run over by a car. The dog's owner, a small girl called Christine cried passionately while her father buried the body. No one at this time was paying attention to Mickey, the father's Labrador. He remained there, contemplating the grave with a strange look.

Later that night, the girl's father was awakened by frantic whining outside the house. When he opened the door, he saw with horror that the sack in which he had buried Percy was lying across the garden path. Nearby he noticed Percy's body and next to it Mickey in a state of mad agitation. Mickey was licking Percy's face and nuzzling his mouth in an evident attempt to give the dead dog the kiss of life. Watching in disbelief this seemingly futile devotion, Christine's father became even more depressed than he had been when he was burying Percy the first time.

Suddenly the dead animal twitched. Then Percy moved his head and whimpered faintly.

Christine and her family were amazed. Somehow Mickey had been able to detect the faint spark of life in an almost dead animal, buried in a deep hole. Clever Mickey was named Pet of the Year by the animal charity Pro-dog, and for the rest of his life he was a local hero.

Dog surgeon

In 1989, a London secretary called Bonita Whitfield became extremely annoyed by the bizarre behaviour of her collie-cross. The dog developed the very unpleasant and embarrassing custom of sniffing the back of one of her legs. Eventually, Bonita became so puzzled by her dog's persistent and weird behaviour that she decided to closely check the back of her leg. To her surprise, she found a small lump but she decided it was just an ordinary mole and soon forgot about it.

Then, one summer's day, while she was working in her garden, the dog tried to bite off the lump on her leg — as if he were a surgeon. To Bonita, it appeared the dog was convinced the lump should not be there and had decided to remove it. Bonita became so perplexed by her dog's strange behaviour that she decided to consult a doctor. As soon as the doctor examined the lump, he sent her to King's College Hospital. There it was diagnosed as a cancerous tumour. It had to be removed that day to try to prevent it spreading to other parts of the body.

When the surgeon who operated on Bonita heard the story about her dog's behaviour, he speculated that her pet must somehow have been able to 'sniff out' the cancer growing in her leg and wanted to warn her.

The specialists at the cancer unit were so impressed by the dog's strange ability that they decided to establish a special research programme to find out whether dogs could be used for early detection of cancer in humans.

Little canine angel

Just before World War I, Ann Wigmore had an accident. She was taken to the nearby Middleboro hospital in Massachusetts, with both legs broken just above the ankles.

Several days later, her mother told Ann, with tears in her eyes, that gangrene had set in and the doctors had decided that the legs must be amputated. To Ann, the situation was not only horrible, but ridiculous. She had seen her grandmother take care of many cases of gangrene in injured villagers. All that was needed was the proper diet and packs of herbs and grass.

Ann did not give her consent for the operation, and she was taken home to die. Her parents were enraged by her refusal. Her father would not speak to her and her mother, through fear of retribution, could only comfort Ann in secret. Her uncle, who was dying of cancer, was her saviour. Every morning he carried Ann into the yard, put her on a bench on the grass and left her there in the sun.

All day Ann reached down and pulled up the long grass and ate copious quantities of it. She was lonely though, the hours passed slowly and she had no companions. She prayed, and an angel appeared from nowhere, a nondescript little white dog with long curly hair. He seemed friendly and companionable.

Each day he lay stretched comfortably in the shade cast by Ann's bench, but never out of patting distance. During the days which followed, Little Angel as Ann called him was her constant companion. Every so often, he left his place in the shade, climbed carefully to the bench, so as not to cause Ann pain, and licked the greenish patches which showed on her thin legs.

This 'dog treatment' continued for some time. Gradually the pain seemed less and the greenish appearance of the flesh seemed to be disappearing. One happy morning a neighbour, a surgeon, stopped by to say hello, as was his custom but when he glanced at Ann's legs, he was visibly surprised by what he saw. The gangrene had disappeared — as the doctors said 'miraculously'.

Dog vet operated on a cat

In 1870, the British press reported the case of a dog who operated on a cat. By mistake, the dog's feline friend swallowed a needle and thread. The needle stuck in his throat and the cat was faced with death.

Carlo, the cat's canine friend, sensed that something was going wrong and immediately came to the cat's rescue. Carlo commenced to lick Dick's neck. The cat held his head aside to give the dog more room. The licking continued, with short intervals, for nearly twenty-four hours. Carlo occasionally paused to press his tongue against his cat friend's neck, as if trying to find something thrust from the inside.

At length, Carlo's whole body quivered with excitement as he tried to catch something with his teeth. As he succeeded he gave a sudden jerk and pulled the needle through the cat's skin where it hung by the thread which still held it from the inside. An onlooker then finished the incredible operation by pulling out the thread. The proud dog looked as if he were saying 'Look what I have done'.

The dog who was better than a human physician

After Victoria Doroshonko of Texas had a serious car accident she became a cripple. As well, she began to suffer from epilepsy. She had up to 24 seizures a day. Death was a constant threat and she could not leave her house or lead a normal life. Victoria required constant care and she became so depressed that she did not want to live. One day though a prison in Washington State where inmates train dogs as companions and aids for disabled people contacted Victoria. Their dogs were trained to open and close doors, pick up the telephone receiver, pull wheelchairs and fetch.

Victoria made a decision to adopt one of the dogs, and this decision saved her life. Two golden retrievers were chosen as her possible companions. One dog showed no interest in Victoria. As soon as he saw her having a seizure he fled.

The other dog, however, immediately showed that he cared. This new pet had a great influence on Victoria's life. Soon her anxiety reduced and she was able to resume attending classes at her local college.

One day, the dog behaved weirdly. He refused to listen to Victoria or to cooperate. The dog only calmed down after his mistress reached her classroom. Five minutes later Victoria was hit by a major epileptic seizure. Evidently somehow the dog knew about the forthcoming seizure and wanted to warn her.

From then on he always warned Victoria about a seizure 15-45 minutes before it struck. Victoria was very happy to have such a talented pet. The relationship and love 'grew and grew' according to Victoria. 'We became like one, like each other's shadow,' she added. Feeling safe again, because of her dog's marvellous ability, Victoria began to socialise and lead a normal life.

Chapter Three

Funny dog stories

Canine cookie monster

Even the cleverest and best mannered dogs sometimes like to make mischief. Possibly the strangest case involved a collie belonging to Fred Gibson, who lived in Atlanta, Georgia. Fred trained the dog to carry a coin to a baker to buy biscuits. One day, however, Fred ran out of coins so gave the dog a written order.

Fred found this method more convenient and began to give the dog a written order whenever he was peckish.

Weeks later, though, when Fred received the baker's bill he became very irate. He then rushed off to the baker, complaining that he had been overcharged. While the two were quarrelling, the dog came into the baker's shop carrying a piece of paper in his mouth.

'Your dog buys all the biscuits,' said the baker.

'But I never gave him an order today,' said Fred.

The shopkeeper took the piece of paper from the dog, and checked it.

It was blank.

Whenever the dog was hungry and wanted to have a biscuit, it seemed, he found a piece of blank paper and carried it to the shop. The baker, accustomed to the written instruction from his client, had never bothered to examine the 'order' brought by the cunning animal.

Strange initiative

A very 'efficient' dog in a London suburb was being taught to pick up the morning paper lying at the gate and bring it into the house. Finally, when the owner found the dog understood his command, he praised him and rewarded him with a very tasty treat. Next morning, to win more of the treat the dog brought home thirty newspapers. He had stolen all the newspapers in the neighbourhood.

Mistaken identity

Valerie and John Collins, an American couple visiting Acapulco in Mexico, took pity on a stray chihuahua. They liked the tiny dog so much they took it back to their hotel and fed it. Next morning, though, their tiny pet was foaming at the mouth. Valerie and John took the animal to a vet. The vet looked over their dog and told them it was a sewer rat infected with rabies.

Dog with four testicles

Disaster struck the over-ambitious Belgian owner of a Dobermann who believed he had an excellent small specimen of the breed and wanted to display him at one of the most prestigious dog-shows in Germany.

He found though that the dog's testicles had failed to descend. This would certainly be regarded by the judges as a fault in an adult dog.

The Belgian was not discouraged, however. He arranged for testicle implants to be put in by a vet. After the scars had healed, the owner proudly took his pet to the show now convinced his dog would win.

The judge who examined the dog soon found to his astonishment that it had four testicles instead of two. The owner hadn't noticed that the dog's own testicles had descended to join the artificial ones a few days before the show. The Belgian and his over-endowed dog were thrown out.

Dog nuptials

Those who think that only humans marry are wrong. In California animals also get married. In fact, in 1986 alone, seventeen animal marriage ceremonies took place. Responsible for formalising unions between animals is Dawn Rogers, a California animal pastor. She has a mail order preacher's licence from the Universal Life Church which entitles her to perform such unusual marriages officially.

The married animals are mainly dogs or cats. But Dawn has also conducted a marriage ceremony for a pair of goldfish and even for frogs. Prices of animal weddings vary, but go as high as $400.

Canine non comprendo

In 1983, police in Wayne, New Jersey, USA, purchased a highly trained German shepherd from Germany. It cost $2800. The New Jersey police soon noticed that the expensive dog never followed their instructions. The dog was not dumb though. Being German, it had been trained to follow instructions in German not English.

Dogs as boomerangs

Hans Roehm bred German shepherds at his kennels in Hamburg; each dog was carefully trained by Roehm himself.

Every time someone purchased one of the dogs, it rushed back to Roehm's kennels as soon as it could. According to police records compiled later, one of Roehm's dogs returned to him from nine different buyers!

Not the most musical dog in the world

The owner of a boxer by the name of Fudge was surprised to hear the strains of 'American Patrol' emanating from the body of his dog at precisely 6.45 a.m. The same bizarre song was repeated at the same time that evening. He later discovered that his dog had swallowed a musical watch.

No use as a hunting dog

One day a boy named Jacek was walking alone in the forest of southern Poland. Suddenly he heard whining. He searched around and soon discovered a tiny brown puppy. Realising that the puppy must have been abandoned by its mother, Jacek decided to take it home.

The boy's parents reluctantly accepted the new pet. But he cried and howled at inappropriate times, especially at night. He woke the whole family. The noise of the puppy at night became so unbearable that Jacek's parents soon insisted that the puppy join the farm animals in the barn.

To everyone's surprise, the puppy enjoyed living in the barn. Soon he even stopped howling. He was always busy observing the other animals. He seemed most interested in the ducks. The mother duck watched the puppy back. Soon, the ducks' mother showed her care for the puppy by putting fresh straw into his box and offering him her own food.

A few days later Jacek was astonished to see his puppy following the mother duck and her children. Soon it became clear that the puppy had started to believe he was a duck. So did the ducks' mother. Whenever the puppy got out of line, the mother duck quacked at him. She even pecked him when he did not obey her commands. This rarely happened though since the dog did his best to be an obedient 'son'.

One day Jacek even saw his puppy-duck together with his 'brothers' and 'sisters' making attempts to fly. Seeing the young ducks flap their wings the puppy flapped his. At first, his 'wings' were his front legs. Then he stood on his hind legs and waved his front ones in the air. When this movement did not work, the dog began kicking backwards with his back legs, all to no avail.

The puppy continued to lead his life as a duck until Jacek's friends arrived one day with their own dog. This was the first dog the puppy-duck had ever seen. At first he treated the interloper as an unknown and dangerous creature. Soon, however, he discovered his affinity with the dog and they began to play. Gradually the puppy-duck abandoned his strange duck status.

Puppy with a very odd bark

One day a trusting young man from northern Italy bought a 'pedigree' puppy from a gipsy. It was a very good deal. The gipsy only wanted $20 for the dog, and the young man was very happy. About a month later, the man began to worry when his new pet refused to bark or yap as dogs do.

He was so upset with the weird behaviour of his puppy that he decided to take it to the local vet. They soon informed him that his puppy was actually a lion cub.

Dog dish with a twist

A British couple sent to work in Hong Kong, on their first night went out to dine in a local restaurant. They had problems communicating with the waiter and it was only after a great deal of sign language they were able to convey to him their choice of meal.

Their pet dog was also hungry, so the next challenge was to explain, using sign language, that their pet also needed some food. The couple pointed to the dog and to their mouths and it seemed that the waiter immediately understood as the dog was led away to the kitchen. After waiting for quite a long time the couple were astounded and horrified when the waiter brought them a large platter, and whipped away the cover to reveal to them their succulently and crisply roasted dog.

Chapter Four

Dogs as thieves and smugglers

Canine pickpocket

Tom Gerrard, a famous eighteenth-century London thief owned a very talented dog called Grip. The dog used his intelligence for very unworthy causes though. Tom had trained his dog to be a thief.

The dog's task was to approach a well-dressed man in the street wagging his tail and wriggling in a friendly manner, trying to persuade the man to pat him.

Usually the stranger, impressed by its friendly behaviour, would bend his head and shoulders forward to stroke the dog. Grip, with his strong sense of smell, could quickly locate the man's leather wallet. With a jerk of the head he suddenly seized the wallet and ran away so quickly that there was no chance of catching him. He kept running until he reached home, to deliver the stolen treasure into Tom's greedy hands.

One day, Tom was caught, and he was hanged soon after. As the grieving dog roamed the streets of London he was spotted by Rev Burgess, a Presbyterian clergyman who took pity on Grip and adopted him.

Soon a great friendship developed between the man and his new pet. Of course problems soon cropped up. One day the reverend popped in to a shop and left the dog outside.

When he came out, Grip gave him a wallet containing some silver and a few coppers. The clergyman thought that his dog must have found a wallet dropped in the street. He advertised, but the owner of the wallet could not be found, so Rev Burgess turned the money over to the church's Poor Box.

Some days later, the reverend paid a pastoral call on a sick parishioner. Grip remained outside but did not remain idle. So when the clergyman returned, the dog presented him with another wallet. This time it was stuffed with bank notes and gold sovereigns. The next day, the faithful dog greeted his master with another wallet.

By now, the clergyman knew something had to be wrong, how could a dog find three wallets lying in the street in only one week. Rev Burgess consulted friends at Scotland Yard. The dog of the famous thief was well known to the officers there, so they were immediately able to verify that indeed the clergyman's new dog was the famous criminal's skilled retriever.

Canine drug smuggler

Workers at New York international airport once discovered an exhausted, sick-looking dog wandering the airport apparently in search of its master. The airport staff handed the dog into the care of vet, Dr Steven Wernstein. While examining the dog, Wernstein did an X-ray which revealed the presence in the dog's stomach of ten condoms full of cocaine. The vet immediately operated on the dog and saved the animal from his dangerous load.

According to Wernstein, there was 2.5 kg of cocaine in the dog's stomach. In honour of the occasion the dog was named Coke.

Investigators later established that he had arrived by plane from Colombia, but it was never discovered who used him for drug smuggling.

Phantom sheep thief

In 1847, John McKenzie a Scot who first migrated to Australia, decided to move to the South Island of New Zealand. There was plenty of free land on the island but John had no money to buy stock.

However, he had a brilliant albeit crooked idea. He decided to train the collie Kellie to steal sheep by droving them to a hidden valley. From the south it could not be seen while to the north only a narrow pass led out of the valley.

John also made sure he had a perfect alibi; it worked like this. John and his dog visited a shepherd who was responsible for a flock of five hundred sheep. During the visit John explained to the dog in Gaelic that he wanted her to take the flock to the valley. Naturally, his host did not understand Gaelic. John merely translated his message as meaning 'You are a good girl'.

After the friendly chat with the shepherd John left the man's house. Soon afterwards John returned alone to the shepherd's house saying: 'I didn't like the look of the weather so I turned back. May I shelter here for the night. I sent my dog home to look after my place, but then she's better protected against the wind and rain than I am. And she can travel a lot faster.'

The shepherd naturally invited his guest to stay overnight. After chatting for a few hours the shepherd went outside to take a look at his sheep before going to bed. He was horrified to see they had all vanished.

John McKenzie acted like a true friend and helped the shepherd to organise a search. The intensive hunt continued for days. Almost everybody was a suspect except John McKenzie since as the shepherd said, 'It couldn't have been Scotch John. He spent the whole night with me.'

John's dog meanwhile did a perfect job. Next morning Kellie moved the flock out again to where John's accomplice was waiting. He then sold the sheep in the Otago market.

Although local shepherds began to maintain a constant guard with mounted armed men, the mysterious disappearances of whole flocks continued. One night, incredibly, the guards noticed a flock of sheep moving in close formation towards the mountains. 'I don't believe it,' exclaimed one guard, 'Sheep travelling at night, and without a shepherd — it's not possible!' The guards decided to go after them, but as they approached the flock it scattered aimlessly across the hillside. When the guards rode away, the sheep closed up again. 'It's a ghost that's driving them — it must be,' said the guards. 'Aye, a phantom, a phantom rustler. What else could drive sheep at night and then disappear into thin air?'

The mysterious sheep disappearances went on for another two years. But one day, the shepherds from Otago discovered that a collie regularly drove flocks of sheep to the market from the south. And the dog resembled the one owned by John McKenzie. Soon the farmers found John's valley where trampled grass indicated that sheep passed there. They also discovered the hidden path to the north.

John was arrested but he did not give up easily. In the courtroom he said: 'No man can say he saw me take a single sheep.'

Sheep passing through his valley did not prove anything. They might have strayed and talking to people from the Otago market was not a crime.

In other words, there was not enough evidence. Then the prosecution brought Kellie in to court and released her. The dog ran to where John stood and leapt at him, licking his hands and face and pawing at his chest. She obviously belonged to John and was rejoicing at their reunion. 'Oh lass, lass. You have surely betrayed me now. I'm as good as sentenced already.' John was condemned to five years imprisonment.

Kellie was not punished though and there was even an attempt to find a Gaelic-speaking shepherd for her. But Kellie refused to work for anyone else. The clever bitch was nevertheless highly valued and her puppies were in demand by sheepmen from all over New Zealand.

Chapter Five

Dog ghosts

Dog ghost saves its owner from death by fire

One day in 1946, while Norma Kresgal was walking in the countryside, she had the strange sensation of not being alone. She stopped and looked around but could not see anyone so she continued on her way. The weird sensation compelled her to leave the road and turn into the nearby forest. Shortly she found a large collie lying on the ground. The dog was wounded, with blood on its fur.

He was too heavy to be carried so Norma ran to fetch assistance. With the help of her father the wounded dog was taken to a local vet who removed a bullet from the dog's throat and saved his life. The collie was adopted by Norma Kresgal and he became the family pet.

The dog only differed from other dogs in that his voice box was permanently damaged by the bullet and he was unable to bark normally. The dog, who they named Corky, lived with the Kresgals for years, until he died and was buried on their farm.

The year after Corky's death the Kresgals moved to New York where they rented an apartment. One night after they had lived in New York for a few months, as Mrs Kresgal recalled: 'I was awoken by a sudden strange sound. It was Corky's hoarse bark. I thought I was dreaming and was about to go back to sleep when I heard him again, loud and clear.' Puzzled by the bark, Mrs Kresgal jumped out of bed and opened the door. Instead of her dog she saw a great cloud of smoke. She aroused her husband and they were able to escape from the fire before it was too late.

Mrs Kresgal later remembered:

'The tears were running down my face. Tom my husband, thinking I was upset about our things being destroyed, told me not to worry because we were insured. He didn't realise I was crying in gratitude, thanking God with all my heart for letting my Corky, come back to us long enough to arouse me — before it was too late.'

The strangest visitor

One summer evening in Poland, a retired school teacher was woken by her cat's yowling. Soon the cat began hissing and spitting as if profoundly terrified. The woman finally decided to get up and investigate. She was convinced that a burglar was in the house. When she went into the hallway she burst into laughter. All she could see was her dachshund. The animals had known each other since they were babies and were always on friendly terms. How could the cat be scared of the dog who was his lifelong pal. The woman admonished her cat, but it kept hissing and spitting at the dog, once so familiar to him and now showing no signs of aggressive behaviour.

The woman's pondering over her cat's strange behaviour was suddenly interrupted by the doorbell. At the door she found the man from next door. She was astounded to see that her neighbour was holding in his arms the limp body of a dachshund that looked precisely like her own dog. The neighbour blurted out: 'I'm sorry but your dog was hit by a car in the street a few minutes ago and he died instantly.'

'It can't be,' she responded furiously but looking closely at the dead dog. She couldn't help noticing the familiar collar and tag. Still unconvinced she looked around the hallway, but now there was no sign of her dog.

She had seen the ghost of her dog. And that was what had frightened her cat.

Hell hound

In Norfolk and Suffolk, England, a phantom dog called Hell Hound is said to have been terrorising the population since the Viking invasions more than one thousand years ago. Locals believe that the Vikings brought him to East Anglia. Whoever sees him will soon die.

The most notorious encounter with the phantom dog took place on a Sunday in August 1557. As night was falling, the terrible dog appeared in the town of Beccles. He burst into a local church during evening service. According to contemporary reports, the phantom dog with its flashing eyes was surrounded by 'fearful flashes of fire'. The people who saw it panicked. Two people were trampled by the crowds escaping from the Church.

The terrible dog was also reported in Blythburgh, a village in Suffolk.

There, the dog suddenly entered the local church causing panic and deaths. The church steeple was reported to have fallen down.

Reports about the Hell Hound, by now known as Black Shuck, continued to appear. In 1939, the London *Evening News* reported the experience of Jimmy Farman, a Norfolk farmer. He saw the phantom dog while he was walking with his own dog: 'A great black dog it was and the eyes were like railway lamps. He crossed my path down by the far dyke. My old bitch almost went mad with fear. Crouched down she did, and the hairs rose up on her back as though they were bristles. For some minutes, I couldn't get her to move, no, not a step and she moaned terribly, just like a child.'

Ghosts of the Isle of Dogs

The Isle of Dogs is the name given to an area on the north side of the Thames within the bend of the river, opposite the Royal Naval College, Greenwich. Now covered in office towers and apartments, the area got its name from the tragic story of a young nobleman.

Long ago the isle was covered by forest and the young man celebrated his wedding day by going there with his wife on a wild boar hunt. His bride was unable to keep up with the hunt and she and her horse were swallowed up by the quick sands and mud of the tidal River Thames. When her husband went to look for her, he too was drowned in the mud.

For centuries after, the marshy forest was believed to be haunted by a human ghost which was accompanied by a pack of ghostly dogs.

Dog ghost saves toddler from drowning

One afternoon, while napping, Walter Manuel of Los Angeles dreamt about his dog Lady who had died three weeks before. In the dream Lady was barking like mad. Walter woke up exhausted by the unpleasant dream and went to the window. As he reached it, he saw his two-year-old son falling into the swimming pool. Thanks to the ghostly barking, he rushed out in time to save his child.

Scotland's canine ghost

Late in the nineteenth century, a particularly frightening ghost haunted Ballechin House, near Logierait in Scotland.

The owner of the house had boasted that after his death he would enter the body of his favourite spaniel and come back to haunt his children.

When the man died in 1874, his family took his declarations seriously. To prevent his return they shot all fourteen of his dogs, including the spaniel.

Soon after, the house was sold. One day, not long after moving in, the wife of the new owner had the sensation of a characteristic doggy smell and the feeling that something was brushing against her. But there were no dogs in the house.

This was just the beginning. Soon, weird crashes and bangs were heard, and unknown voices began to haunt the house. For the next twenty years this went on, and nothing could be done to stop it.

In 1887 Lord Bute, a connoisseur of psychic occurrences rented the haunted house and invited a number of researchers to investigate the strange phenomena. The invited guests were told all the stories about the extraordinary sounds and visions experienced by former occupants. The researchers were themselves able to record all the extraordinary happenings in the house. One night, for example, a Pomeranian dog woke the researchers with its desperate barking. The dog had found two disembodied black paws pressed to the top of a table.

The haunted house was finally demolished because the owner could no longer stand the incredible events which the dog's ghost was believed to be causing.

Chapter Six

Dogs in history, rituals and beliefs

Christ depicted as a dog-god

Gnostic sects which superimposed Christian doctrine on pagan religious teachings sometimes combined figures of dog-gods with those of Christ. Their gems had images of the dog-god with arms outstretched in the form of a crucifix. Graffiti found on the wall of a Roman house depicted a dog-headed man holding a cross with a devotee worshipping him.

Marriage of a human to a dog

The Gonds of Bastar (Central India) believe that it is necessary for a woman to marry a dog if the woman's husband has been killed by a tiger and she wishes to marry again. They believe that the husband's spirit has entered the tiger's body and will try to kill any new man she marries. The solution to the problem is for the widow first to ritually marry a dog. The first husband's jealous spirit will then be satisfied by killing the dog and will spare the life of the new human husband.

Christian dog saints

In early Christian Europe saints were often depicted in the form of dogs or were shown as human with a dog's head.

St Dominic and St Bernard were both sometimes represented in the form of a dog.

The Byzantine St Christopher was depicted as a young man with the head of a dog.

This came about, according to legend, because St Christopher was a very handsome young Roman soldier. He was so attractive that he was in constant trouble with suitors of both sexes. Young Christopher prayed that he would become ugly and free from temptation. His prayer was answered one day, and his head immediately changed into that of a dog.

A cult based on a legend about the martyrdom of a greyhound evolved in Europe about 1260. The legend had it that a greyhound sacrificed his life to save his master from attack by a deadly snake. The dog's grateful owner buried him in a special tomb.

Soon, the faithful dog became famous in the area and came to be called St Guinefort. Parents began to bring their sick children to the grave of the famous dog in hope of miraculous cures.

Despite determined efforts by priests to eliminate this bizarre cult of a dog, it survived into the twentieth century.

Dog who delayed science history

Sir Isaac Newton, the great mathematician, was working late at night, writing down important new ideas and mathematical computations, the results of years of hard work. His canine friend, Diamond, was sleeping nearby.

Suddenly, the dog woke to hear his master talking with someone at the front door. To protect Sir Isaac, in case his security was endangered, the dog tried to get out of the room, but the door was closed. The dog was furious. He wildly ran around the room, barking. In his excitement, the dog accidentally jolted the table leg and knocked the burning candle over on to the papers. The room was hardly damaged, but Sir Isaac's scientific papers were completely destroyed. Perhaps the great scientist could have been angry. But he did not even contemplate getting rid of the dog or punishing him. Sir Isaac Newton realised the damage caused by his pet was unintentional and that the dog in fact had tried to protect him. Thus, instead of scolding his pet, he patted it and went to bed as if nothing had happened.

The great mathematician had to begin working all over again, and thus some of his important discoveries were significantly delayed.

Dog as humanity's father

In Greenland, a dead child's body was customarily buried with the head of a dog. This was done to ensure that the child's ghost would have a reliable guide in the afterworld.

According to some Greenland beliefs a dog was the ancient father of the whole human family.

Dog priests of contemporary India

At a temple in Dharwar in northern India, members of a Dravidian sect worship a dog-god. The temple priests dress in blue woollen coats and they have bells and dog skins tied around their waists.

They look strange and their behaviour is most unusual. When they meet pilgrims at the entrance to the temple, they bark and howl like real dogs. Each priest has a bowl in which pilgrims place milk and food offerings.

The priests' weird behaviour is not confined to making dog-like sounds. Imitating their dog, the priests quarrel like dogs over the food left for them in the bowls. Without using their hands they pick up in their mouths any food which is spilt on the temple floor.

Dog sorceresses of contemporary Japan

In rural Japan, there are still women said to be sorceresses, with dog-spirits. Although the women are not evil by nature, they are not always able to control the dog-spirit which sometimes independently inflicts harm.

In houses where such women live there is always a monument to the dog spirit. Offerings are regularly made to the image in order to appease the dog-spirit and keep it happy. In the past, a dog's head was buried beneath the monument.

A woman who possesses the dog-spirit is believed to be able to cause sickness or kill her enemies. Some villagers claim that when the dog-spirit is released in the house to inflict harm, it utters weird noises.

The dog-spirit is believed to be inherited through the female line, so that the daughter-in-law can take it after her mother-in-law. Sometimes it is not a person but a building which carries the dog-spirit. It is said to be very dangerous for people to fight in such a house.

When a victim discovers that he is sick because of the dog-spirit he must immediately visit a Kitoshi (male sorcerer) for a cure.

Weird undertaker

In ancient Persia, the dog was regarded as a protector of humans and a shepherd of animal flocks. According to the decree of Ormuz, killing dogs was a crime and people had a duty to cherish them. Ancient Persians respected their dogs so much that their most important and wise men were called Khan, meaning dog.

Dogs were also linked with the burial of the dead. Ancient Persians delayed burials until the bodies had been ripped apart by dogs. Poor people used the village's stray dogs, while wealthier people employed their own household dogs for this purpose.

Dog Shogun

Seventeenth century Japanese Shogun Tsunayoshi loved dogs above any humans in the world. He was known as the Dog Shogun. He cared for 100,000 dogs. In order to raise money to feed them all he imposed an unpopular new tax on farmers. As a result there was galloping inflation and trouble for the treasury. The Dog Shogun also passed a law stating that all dogs in Japan must be treated kindly and addressed using the most polite language.

Dogs as Greek soldiers

In ancient Greece large dogs were often used in war. They were especially trained, and fought in squadrons. Several times the dogs proved vital to the outcome of a battle. In Corinth once, the canine guards were on duty on the ramparts of the city while their masters slept off lengthy celebrations and drinking. But enemy troops made a surprise attack on the city.

The dogs heard them approaching and set upon the enemy. It was an uneven fight, but the faithful dogs fought bravely till death. Eventually, all the dogs were killed except one. But the fighting dogs had made such a noise that they woke the garrison just in time for them to defend the city.

When Philip of Macedon won a battle against the Thracians, the Thracians escaped into the forest, and Philip was only able to hunt them down with the help of his war dogs.

War dogs of ancient Rome

In ancient Rome, dogs were used for communication during war. Dogs trained for this purpose were forced to swallow a metal tube containing secret messages. When the dog-messenger reached its destination, having run through the lines, and often wounded, it was not praised for the valuable service though. The dog was killed so the message could be extracted from its bowels.

Ancient Romans also employed war-trained 'devouring dogs'. To make them more ferocious the dogs were refused food for several days before a battle.

Roman war-mastiffs often had their own special armour and knives fastened to their collar, back and sides. An armoured dog like this could inflict severe cuts on the legs of enemy horses in battle.

The Romans often attached torches to the war-dogs and sent them in front of the cavalry to frighten enemy horses and disrupt cavalry charges. Mastiffs were even used to attack and scare enemy elephants which were used in battles to carry teams of archers.

Dogs in World Wars

Dogs were used extensively in both World Wars. At the outbreak of World War I Germany had six thousand Alsatians fully trained and twenty thousand dogs were sent into battle over the next four years.

During the war, seven thousand British dogs were killed in action. The French sent ten thousand dogs to the front and in addition used eight thousand sledge dogs in the Vosges mountains.

During World War II Germany employed an enormous number of dogs. Some two hundred thousand were used just to guard concentration camps.

There was a special war dog school in Britain; the US

army sent trained dogs into the jungle to find wounded and flush out snipers. In Norway the Defence Minister was empowered to order mobilisation of all privately owned elkhounds as sledge dogs for the war effort.

Dogs were also specially trained during World War II to detect mines. In fact dogs are still being used in this way nowadays for detection of terrorist bombs.

Japanese dog-gods

Some of the many Japanese and Chinese mountain-gods were dogs. At Chichibu in Japan a dog-deity was the protector of a mountain and two sacred dogs, one black and one white, were always in attendance at the dog's shrine. The dog-deity received homage and sacrifices from pilgrims.

A special temple was built in Japan for a god who was patron of all dogs. Inside the temple there were hundreds of lamps, and a priest struck the temple's bells with iron hammers shaped like a dog's head. A large white marble dog was worshipped on the altar dedicated to this god.

The dog was also worshipped in the sixteenth-century Shinto temple on the mountain called 'Dog's Head and Tail.' This shrine was built to commemorate the dog who saved his owner's life when he was attacked by a deadly snake, but was accidentally beheaded by his master as he slashed off the snake's head.

Dog temple in China

In a well known temple outside the city of Foochow in China is an image of a large dog; children put cakes, biscuits and bread into its mouth and then remove them and eat them as a preventive remedy against colic.

Multiheaded monster dog

Ancient Greeks believed that a monstrous multiheaded dog called Cerberus guarded the entrance to Hell. Heroes of Greek legends had to come up with ingenious ways of getting past this cruel canine monster. When Orpheus was looking for Eurydice, he charmed the monster with his flute-playing, and Aeneas had to drug the monster with honey cake soaked in drugs.

Oppressed English dogs

The Viking conqueror of England, Canute, introduced the so-called Forest Laws, which made illegal the owning of hunting dogs by commoners. This made hunting most difficult. Only 'freemen' that is, people somewhat elevated on the social scale, were allowed to keep greyhounds. And even these dogs had to be mutilated to make them incapable of hunting. The mutilation took various forms. At first the dog's knees were cut. Later, this method was replaced by cutting the ball of the foot. Finally it was sufficient to crush three claws.

For centuries, there was no attempt by rulers of England to repeal these cruel laws, considered to be so unjust by their subjects. Even if a small dog ran after a deer, in harmless fun, the dog's owner was severely punished.

In the Middle Ages, owning a dog could be regarded as grounds for an accusation of poaching, and until the reign of Richard I (1157-99), the penalty for poaching was castration, blinding or cutting off hands and feet. The Forest Laws concerning dog ownership applied until 1688.

Canine church attendance

During the Middle Ages, dogs went to church with their masters on a regular basis. In fact, special pews were kept at the back of churches for shepherds and their dogs.

In the town of Tadlow, on Christmas Day 1638, a dog approached the communion table and took the bread prepared for the holy sacrament in his mouth and rushed away with it.

To prevent such incidents, the Bishop of Norwich ordered that a rail be put before the communion table in each church so that no dog could pass.

For several centuries dogs were widely used as foot-warmers in churches. Special dog-minders kept the dogs under control.

In contemporary Adelaide, South Australia, dogs and other pets regularly attend services at one of the local churches.

Doggie bag with a difference

In the early days of European settlement, the Sandwich Islanders (Hawaiians) loved dogs and ate them.

They too treated dogs like children, carrying them if a road was muddy or rough.

The Chinese ate dogs, and dog meat was a major source of protein there. It was more an occasional delicacy than a staple food. The Chinese bred dogs specifically for eating. To make them tastier, they were fed an entirely vegetable diet.

Until recently eating dog was still widespread in China though only among the poor. In the late Nineteenth century the flesh of black dogs (and cats) was displayed outside Cantonese restaurants.

Dogs and magic

Some races believed that by eating dogs they would acquire their bravery and shrewdness. Indians of South Dakota were such enthusiastic dog eaters that their tribe was known as 'dog-liver eaters'. They ate the raw liver of freshly slaughtered dogs.

At the beginning of the rite a dog with its legs bound was thrown into the middle of a group of dancing people. The dog was then slaughtered by the medicine-man. He then extracted its liver, cut it into strips and then hung the dog's carcase on a pole. The people danced around the pole, grimacing and smacking their lips, and one by one each man grabbed a portion of the liver in his teeth. The liver had to be eaten when fresh and warm.

Dog aristocrats

Three thousand years ago there was a cult of the pekinese in Chinese courts. The dogs were bred and looked after by eunuchs. As there was a low regard for girls in ancient China, baby girls were often killed so the puppies could be suckled by the mothers. Puppy suckling was supervised by the emperor himself.

There were about one thousand eunuchs living in the palace and each of them wanted to present the emperor with the finest dog. To achieve their goal they devised many methods of interfering with the natural growth of the puppies. To try to make them smaller than usual, puppies were often enclosed in tight-fitting wire cages until they reached adulthood.

Another approach was to eliminate all opportunities for exercise after the third month to reduce sharply the pups' appetites. Some eunuchs held the puppies for days on end by gentle pressure of their fingers to exaggerate the width between their shoulders. To cause short noses, the cartilages of puppies just a few days old were broken with nails, chopsticks or thumbnails. Noses of some pekes were massaged daily to restrain their growth.

Those pekes that the emperor liked best were taken into the ranks of the highest mandarins and called princes or dukes. They were so respected that state officers paid them homage. The dogs had personal servants, and imperial guards kept watch over them. After the daily bath these pekinese were sprayed with perfume by servants and laid to rest on silken cushions. Adult pekinese were given regular exercise and carried around in special palanquins. These dogs were the constant companions of the emperor and his ladies. The dogs could be seen sleeping on the imperial couch, sitting in front of the emperor's saddle, or even beside him on the throne.

Draught dogs of Britain

Draught dogs were once common in Britain. They could be seen pulling carts, laden with meat, fish, milk and other goods. Fisherfolk used to carry fish from the coast up to the London markets using teams of four draught dogs. They could pull heavy loads of three or four hundredweight.

In those days long teams of dogs pulled travelling shows from one country fair to another.

In Sussex there was a team of postal dogs which carried mail between Steyning and Storrington.

Dog as messenger to the gods

Dog sacrifice has been practised in many parts of the world. Some races claimed that a dog could be used as a messenger to the gods. The Iroquois Indians at the sacrificial festival, celebrated annually over many centuries, used to send to their Great God, the spirit of a white dog with a petition. This sacrifice was preceded by four days of religious observances during which priests visited each home urging the inhabitants to clean their houses and to leave all their sorrows behind.

On the day of the festival, people dressed in brilliantly coloured clothes. The sacrificial dog selected had to be entirely white and free from blemishes. First it was smeared with red paint and tied up with ribbons of various colours. A written message to the Great God was then tied to a bunch of feathers and fastened to the dog's neck.

The sacrificial dog was then placed on a funeral pyre. Before the pyre was set alight the dog was strangled. Following the rite the ashes of the dog were collected and scattered at the doors of all the houses in the community.

Japanese dog-charms and talismans

Dog-charms were very popular in Japan. In a Tokyo temple there was a special service twice a month for pregnant women and whenever the service coincided with a dog-day, dog-charms could be purchased at the temple. Dog-charms were said to ensure easy delivery.

During the fifth month of pregnancy it was customary for Japanese women to put on special girdles and a dog-day was always chosen for this important ritual.

The most widespread Japanese dog-charm was the inu-hariko, a papier-mâché dog-box. These objects had the body of a sleeping dog and a child's face. The dog-box was white with black dots and often covered in red and gold cloth.

The inu-hariko used to be offered as a wedding gift; the parents of the bride placed it by the married couple's bed. Next day a go-between returned it to the parents who preserved it as a guarantee of luck.

The inu-hariko box was commonly used in lying-in rooms. Cotton wool, napkins, powder, brushes and bandages were kept in it. Before the birth the dog-box was dressed in the baby's first clothes, which were given to the baby when it was born.

The Japanese character for 'dog' was often written on a baby's forehead to protect it against an evil bird which it was thought could enter a home at night and steal the baby's soul.

When older children were taken for a walk at night, the 'dog' character was also written in red ink on their foreheads to guard them against evil influences and especially against fox and badger-demons.

Dog deity of ancient Egypt

The ancient Egyptians worshipped the god Anubis. He was represented by the figure of a man with the head of a jackal.

Anubis guarded cemeteries, presided over tombs and was the god of embalming. He was also Guardian of the Scales of Truth. He supervised the weighing of a vase representing the actions of the deceased in one scale against the figure or emblem of truth in the other.

Hermanubis, the Alexandrian dog-deity, had most of the characteristics of Anubis. This god was also shown as a human with a dog's head. The primary duty of Hermanubis was to guide souls of the dead through the underworld. This god was sometimes called the 'pregnant one' and was regarded as a protector of pregnant women. He was also shown in love charms worn by men.

The god's temple in Alexandria housed silver figures of Hermanubis and gold libation bowls. Ingots of gold were offered to him.

The dog-god's temple resembled a large kennel because it housed dogs sacred to the god. Priests fed the dogs and took care of them. To imitate the dog-god priests wore wooden dog-masks with black muzzles and ears and black stripes drawn across their neck. The dog-god's priests carried in procession a huge statue of the black canine-god. The statue's mouth, ears, eyelids, nostrils and mane were of gold. The statue was dressed in white linen grave clothes since it was a funeral deity.

The Egyptian city of Cynopolis was the centre of a dog cult. Dogs were ritually fed on food which was donated by the city's inhabitants.

If a dog died from natural causes, members of the household were obliged to shave their heads and bodies, and had to throw away any food present in the house at the time of the dog's death.

Dog funeral rites were performed with solemn ceremony. The burial of the dog which guarded the Pharaoh of Egypt was performed with a ceremony worthy of a great man. The Pharaoh himself presented the dog with an elegant coffin and the tomb for the dog was specially made by the best royal craftsmen.

In Cynopolis dogs' bodies were prepared for burial by embalmers. When the embalmed body of the dog was deposited in its tomb, mourners lamented loudly and beat their chests. The wooden coffin in which the dog-mummy was placed was often in the shape of a dog. On the surface of the coffin a figure of a dog was made with eyes of obsidian or glass.

In many other Egyptian towns there were special graveyards for dog-mummies.

Dogs in exorcism

In ancient China even dog blood was believed to have supernatural powers. The blood was said to give strong powers of exorcism.

From AD 676 onwards four dogs were sacrificed annually to expel spirits causing fever and to ward off calamity and disease. Later, sacrifices were reduced to one white dog which was ritually killed every new year. Its blood was splashed over the gates of Beijing to ward off evil spirits and to prevent misfortune.

In order to expel malignant evil spirits Chinese doctors used to kill a black dog, collect its blood in a bowl and sprinkle it around the house. One remedy against evil forces included the following procedure: the walls of the whole house were smeared either with blood or gall from black dogs.

In north-eastern India the custom involving annual sacrifice of dogs saw the dogs ceremonially slaughtered at the gate of the village. The dogs' heads were then set on poles.

Dog worship in Peru

The ancient Huancas of Peru worshipped images of dogs in temples. Surprisingly, they were also enthusiastic dog eaters. They demonstrated their great devotion to their god-dog by making a kind of trumpet out of the dog's head. They played it during feasts and dances in honour of their dog-god.

In parts of Peru, as a sign of respect, a priest was called 'Alco' meaning dog.

Dog sacrifice in Scandinavia

Before they became Christians, the people of Denmark had the most unusual dog custom. Every ninth year at the winter solstice they sacrificed ninety-nine dogs.

It was even harder for dogs in pre-Christian Sweden. There, on nine consecutive days, ninety-nine dogs were sacrificed. These ritual dog killings were believed to prolong the life of the monarch.

Chinese dog talismans and charms

Lion-dogs standing at the entrance to the imperial palaces in Beijing were the largest talismanic dogs in the world. They were placed there to protect the palaces from attack by evil spirits.

In dynastic China, various precious materials such as amber, ivory and jade had the image of the lion-dog carved on them and were worn or carried about in the belief that they would bring good luck.

According to a book written in AD 752 in China, dog protection was also employed in the following way: 'If a baby cries at night immediately take the hair beneath the throat of a dog, put it into a red bag, and bind it on the hands of the baby. The child stops crying at once.'

Dog battles with elephant

Alexander the Great once received a large dog as a present from the king of Albania. Alexander was very disappointed with the dog though because it refused to fight with bears. He ordered that the dog be killed. When the Albanian king heard about this, he explained in a letter to Alexander that the dog was not a coward, but it refused to fight because the adversary was too feeble. He wrote that such a big dog would only fight with beasts as strong as an elephant or a lion. To prove the point, the king sent Alexander another large dog like the one he had killed.

Alexander was truly amazed; the new dog killed an elephant and a lion in single combat. Alexander then became greatly attached to the dog and when it died, he ordered a special temple in its honour.

Dog Mass

Every year, on 3 November, at Ardennes a hunt mass was celebrated under the name of the 'Mass of St Hubert'. It was commonly referred to as the 'Mass of the dogs'. This custom spread to neighbouring areas. At Chantilly the Mass of the dogs was celebrated until recently. The castle was decorated with flowers spread over the floor and over the kennels.

Prior to the Mass there was a procession of dogs to the chapel. It was led by the community's oldest man, followed by the oldest dog. In the procession came the great dignitaries of the kennels.

When all the dogs were lined up before the portrait of St Hubert, Mass was celebrated. After Mass the priest praised the great saint of the hunt. The assembled people offered prayers to protect all hunting dogs from 'bites, stings, wounds and rabies'. The priest then blessed the hunt and all the hounds.

Chapter Seven

Stories of dogs who save people

The baby who turned into a dog

A two year-old baby lying abandoned in a slum in Manila, Philippines was not noticed by most people. Others passed by unconcerned, and preoccupied with their own problems of survival. The child would soon die from starvation.

Luckily, a dog was more humane than all the humans in the neighbourhood. A mongrel bitch noticed the abandoned baby and immediately knew what to do. She began to suckle the baby. He enthusiastically drank the canine milk. Some locals noticed the canine mother and her adopted human baby and wanted to separate them but the canine mother did not trust human good intentions. She remembered well how they treated the baby previously.

If anyone approached the bitch, they were snarled off. The dog was persistent in her efforts to care for the baby and generally speaking the humans were not that interested.

The dog suckled the baby every day for more than a year. The child eventually began to behave like a dog. Only after many months was it decided that the infant would be taken to a rehabilitation centre.

Vigi saves his master from starvation

King Olaf I of Norway was a very cruel Scandinavian ruler before he converted to Christianity. His ideology was simply 'might makes right'.

When Olaf raided Ireland, his men captured hundreds of cattle. One Irish farmer begged the king to give him back his twenty cows since otherwise his children would starve.

The King responded cynically, making fun of the poor fellow. 'Very good, my man, pick your own twenty out of that mass - pick them correctly - and you shall have them.' The king believed that to be an impossible task. However, the Irishman was not at all discouraged. He whistled and immediately Vigi a shaggy big hound bounded up to him. The farmer said something in Gaelic and the dog began searching for his master's cows among the hundreds assembled there. In a matter of minutes all twenty of the farmer's own cows were herded in front of the king. The king was so impressed that he bought the dog from the farmer for a heavy gold bracelet.

The king and Vigi became inseparable friends. He was always in the company of the dog; they did nearly everything together and a number of times the dog saved his life. When Olaf died, Vigi starved himself to death, unable to overcome his immense grief.

A tragic mistake

Gelert was the finest hound owned by King John of England. To win the loyalty of Llewellyn, the most powerful of Welsh princes, the king gave him his daughter in marriage and for a wedding gift they received Gelert.

When the prince's first son was born the hound became the baby's constant guardian. Llewellyn was pleased to have such a reliable guard for his child, for he had began to quarrel with the king who threatened to strike at the prince through his son.

One day a wolf sneaked in to the nursery while the baby was asleep. The dog challenged the wolf and they began to fight.

Later, Llewellyn returned from a hunt. When he entered the nursery he saw the baby's face and clothes smeared with blood. The baby looked as if he were dead. Over the cot stood the dog, blood dripping from his injured jaws.

To Llewellyn, it appeared that Gelert, mad with rabies, had murdered the baby. Llewellyn immediately hacked Gelert into pieces with his long-bladed knife. No sooner had he finished, than Llewellyn heard the baby cry out. He searched around and found the mutilated body of the wolf sprawled behind the cot.

It was only then that the prince realised the dog had saved the life of his son who was not dead but only sleeping. Brave Gelert was buried with almost royal honours by the grateful and ashamed father.

Dog who gave his life

Canadian Andre Mirette owned a cross-breed by the name of Spot, who was his baby son Jean's closest companion and guardian. One day Andre's mother left the pram and baby outside in the sun, not far from the house.

Suddenly, three wolves appeared. The dog knew he would not be able to win a fight with them. The easiest option would be to run away to the safety of the house, leaving the baby to the wolves who would certainly devour him. However, to save the baby, the dog applied a clever strategy. But he had to sacrifice his own life in the process. Spot knew if he ran to the forest the wolves would then turn their attention solely on him. Spot knew that he would not be able to escape from the wolves but he also knew that when the wolves caught him they would be a safe distance from the baby.

Thus, the dog gave his own life to save the baby.

Dogs prevent epidemic

In January 1925, there was a diphtheria outbreak in Nome, Alaska. City health officials were horrified to find their serum supply was insufficient to prevent an epidemic which would kill hundreds. The nearest centre of supply was 960 km away but weather conditions were so awful that they had to rule out bringing the serum by plane.

The desperate officials decided to deploy a relay team of sled dogs. The fastest team was led by a black long-haired malamute called Balto. This 'super-canine' led his team through Alaska and across the frozen Bering Sea under conditions difficult to imagine; 130 km/h blizzards; temperatures often down to −50°C, and very poor visibility.

The remarkable dog could hardly see anything, but he always managed to scent a trail. The dogs ran across enormous snowdrifts. They had to move across tracts of splintered ice that cut the dogs feet like sharp glass.

For much of the trip the human crew were forced to totally rely on the incredible skills of Balto. And Balto's team was the first to reach the destination. It was also the first team to return. The anti-toxin was delivered on 2 February at exactly 5.36 a.m. to the enormous relief of the inhabitants of Nome.

The canine heroes were honoured with a statue of Balto which can be seen in Central Park, New York. The description reads: 'Dedicated to the indomitable spirit of the sled dogs that relayed anti-toxin 600 miles over rough ice, treacherous waters, through Arctic blizzards from Nemana to the relief of stricken Nome in the winter of 1925. Endurance, Fidelity, Intelligence.'

Great canine rescuer

One of the greatest of the St Bernard rescue breed was a Swiss dog named Barry. During his working life, between 1800 and 1812, this dog saved more than forty people from death in the Swiss Alps. The hospice in which the famous dog lived was established by St Bernard of Menton in 1049. From 1750 the hospice rescue dogs saved the lives of over 2500 people.

The most incredible case of Barry's successful life-saving career concerned a young boy who lay unconscious and half frozen under an avalanche. The boy's mother was already dead.

Barry was able to discover the missing boy without human assistance. And he knew what to do. First he lay across the boy's body to restore body heat and then he started licking the boy's face. He continued this until the boy had regained consciousness and was fit enough to climb on to the dog's back. The canine rescuer carried the boy through deep snowdrifts all the way to the nearest monastery where he was given medical treatment.

Barry was also a great psychic. A number of times he was able to predict dangerous snowstorms and avalanches and thus warn people of potential death in the mountains.

When the famous dog retired he was taken to Berne where he died in 1814. His body was stuffed and the famous canine rescuer can still be seen today at the Berne National History Museum.

World War heroes

In World War I an entire British battalion was saved by a specially trained messenger dog, called Airedale Jack. The battalion in France was on the verge of being totally destroyed under a ferocious enemy barrage which cut off all normal communications. Only reinforcements could save them. Their only means of communicating with headquarters was to send the dog with a message.

Airedale Jack had to run four miles close to the ground under intensive fire. Within the first mile his lower jaw was smashed by shrapnel. Soon his body was wounded along its entire length and his front paw was broken into pieces. Yet the wounded dog did not stop; he dragged himself along in an effort to reach his destination. He delivered the message, hidden in a leather pouch on his collar, and died at the commander's feet. The battalion was saved.

Another great dog hero was Bobs, the fox terrier ship's pet on HMS *Tornado*, a vessel which was suddenly attacked by German submarine.

The ship was sinking. Ten men were lying unconscious in a life raft and would certainly die but the clever little dog saved their lives by his persistent barking which was loud enough to attract attention of the crew of nearby HMS *Radiant*.

In 1943, during World War II a shepherd/collie/husky cross named Chips went to Sicily as part of the K-9 corps. The dog and his handler PFC John R. Rowell were involved in battle by the 3rd Division Infantry Regiment of General Patton's 7th Army. The US force was pinned down by an enemy machine-gun post which was extremely difficult to reach. Chips was set loose and ordered to take the post. Attacking alone, the clever dog jumped at the throats of the unsuspecting enemy gunners and forced them to surrender.

Austrian dog hero

One day a shivering, starving puppy entered the officers' mess at the Vienna cavalry barracks. An officer brutally yelled to one of the military stewards to kick the dog out. A captain by the name of Karl Weiss came to the poor animal's aid. He picked up the stray pup and took it to his quarters. He adopted the puppy and named it Hans.

The dog was a mongrel and it was surprising that Karl

adopted such an undistinguished dog. Other officers competed among themselves about how expensive were the blueblooded thoroughbreds they owned.

Karl Weiss was not an ordinary man though. He had few mates and few close friends. Soon the man and the dog became great pals.

The following summer when Weiss's regiment went to the front, he took his dog with him. During a battle the dog was always tied to Weiss's tent.

One day Captain Weiss did not return from battle and was reported missing. Despite a thorough search of the whole battlefield he could not be found among the dead.

Suddenly, Weiss's servant had a brilliant idea. He untied Hans and ordered 'Master! Find Master!' The dog immediately rushed off, with the soldiers after him. Hans soon stopped at a heap of corpses. He began scratching furiously at the topmost bodies as if trying to dislodge them, yelping. The men quickly found Captain Weiss but he looked dead; he was taken to the nearest field hospital where the medical staff revived him.

For seven more years, Captain Weiss and his dog Hans led a happy life. Then Captain Weiss was again reported missing in another battle. Once again the dog led the rescuers to his master. This time, however, the doctor found the captain's wounds to be fatal and he was told that he had only a few more days to live.

After his master's death, the faithful dog stopped eating and starved himself to death.

The dog and the toddler

A toddler once wanted to help his pet collie. One day when his parents were out the three-year-old boy noticed that the dog was hungry. He thought it would be a good idea to prepare a meal for him.

The boy went to the kitchen and moved a stool to the stove, clambered up, took some matches and began to attempt to light the gas. As he had no experience in using matches, tragedy soon struck. The boy's pyjamas caught fire and the terrified boy screamed in agony. His dog responded immediately as if formally trained in first-aid. He knocked the boy to the floor and started rolling over his body in an effort to smother the flames with his own body. The clever dog was soon able to extinguish the fire and saved the boy's life. Although the poor child suffered some burns he soon recovered completely.

Mother gives her child for canine adoption

In 1990 in South Africa, it was discovered that Linda Henricksen, 32, had given to her dog Skaapie full responsibility for the care of her son, Danny. She admitted that she had purposely left her son in the kennel to be raised by her dog. Being alcoholic, she was always so drunk that she found it impossible to care for the child herself.

The boy was found when he was 2 years old. He was naked, very thin and weighed half the normal weight for his age. He behaved like a dog. He moved around on four limbs and whined and barked like a dog. There were signs on the boy's neck that seemed to have been made by the dog-mother's collar. She was a very devoted parent and she died two weeks after the boy was taken away from her.

The dog and the bear

When eight-year-old Romana Strasser was playing ball one day in the farmyard of her home in Austria, she did not anticipate that she would soon be brutally attacked and that her very life would be at risk.

Nor did her father imagine that his 320 kg prize pedigree bear might be strong enough to knock down the gate of his pen. However, this is precisely what happened. The powerful beast smashed the gate and then attacked the man's daughter and threw her to the ground. The bear sank his tusks into the girl's hip and slashed the flesh up to her shoulder. The girl's screams of terror and horrifying pain were heard by the family's five-year-old Alsatian who immediately rushed to the scene. The dog jumped on to the back of the rampaging bear and grabbed its ear, forcing it to lift its head and release its victim.

In this manner the brave dog saved the life of the girl. No doubt, without the dog's swift and courageous action the girl would have died.

Saving one's murderer

Malakoff was a Newfoundland breed dog owned by a wholesale jeweller in Paris. The dog loved to make practical jokes which did not seem funny to many people. This created endless problems. His favourite prank was to get between a pedestrian's legs and send him off balance into the gutter and mud.

The jeweller had several apprentices who hated the dog and his tricks. One day an opportunity cropped up to get rid of the dog.

The dog entered the shop, bleeding and worn out, perhaps from a beating. Jacques, one of the apprentices, bribed a friend to pretend to be a vet and to tell the jeweller that his dog must be put to death at once. Jacques' friend explained to the jeweller that the dog must be killed because he had rabies and any minute would start biting humans.

The jeweller quickly agreed. Jacques put a rope around the dog's neck from one side and another apprentice lassoed it from the other side. The poor animal was then dragged to the end of the nearest pier jutting out into the icy river which was also in flood.

Jacques then tied a large stone to the rope and fastened its free end around the dog's neck. They coiled one of the ropes tightly around Malakoff's front legs. Jacques then pushed the poor animal into the water. Suddenly, the rope broke loose and wound itself around Jacques' ankle, pulling him into the icy water. He could not swim and it seemed that he would drown, too.

And it also became evident that everyone had underestimated Malakoff's swimming talent. He started swimming to the shore, dragging the stone with him. But when noticing Jacques' head disappearing beneath the surface, he swam to his would-be murderer and grabbing him by the coat collar, began hauling him to the bank.

Although the dog understood enough about Jacques' role in the execution attempt he still did his best to save him. It was a very hard swim, Malakoff was weakened by blood loss and cold.

If he had not attempted to save Jacques he would have easily reached the bank.

Eventually, Malakoff was not making any progress at all. A cross-current was pulling them back toward the middle of the river. But never for an instant did Malakoff abandon the man who had tried to kill him.

At last help arrived. People in a row boat reached the man and the dog and both were saved.

Jacques never forgot the dog's deed and he told everybody about the dog. So did the other apprentices who witnessed the incident.

Chapter Eight

Man and dog friendship

Most faithful Japanese dog

Shibuya, the busy Tokyo commuter railway station, is famous for its statue of Hachiko, Japan's most famous dog. Hachiko's master, Professor Elibura Ueno lectured at the Imperial University in the 1920s. Every morning Hachiko went to the station to see his master off. Every evening he went again to meet him as he returned from work.

One day in 1925 Professor Ueno had a fatal heart attack. Not knowing about his death Hachiko went to the station as usual. But his master did not turn up. Eventually he went away but returned to the station the following evening at the appropriate time. In fact, Hachiko never gave up hope that his master would come home. He kept going to the station every evening for 11 years until his own death.

Most faithful dog in the world

Fido, an Italian mongrel who lived in the Tuscan village of Borso San Lorenzo, achieved a canine record. It was the dog's custom to meet his master every day as he returned home from his job in Florence. One afternoon in 1943, Fido's owner was killed in a bombing raid on Florence. The dog went as usual to the bus stop to meet his master, but this time did not find him. The faithful dog did not give up and for more than fifteen years, he went to the same bus stop every day in the hope that he would find his master there. He continued until he died. This was the longest dog vigil ever recorded. The villagers who witnessed the unusual behaviour of the dog decided in 1958 to erect a memorial to Fido to honour his remarkable devotion to his master.

The mayor of the community was also to present the dog with a specially made gold medal. However, just as the mayor was about to hang the medal round Fido's neck, the dog rushed away. It was the time for his master's bus to come.

Dog commits suicide on the death of her master

Jean Ricard of Nice in France, had a mongrel called Coco. They had a close relationship but nobody realised the depth of the dog's love of her master.

Jean, at the age of 59, had a fatal heart attack. The dog's response to this tragic event was terrible. For a week, she refused to be moved from the balcony of the neighbour's fourth floor apartment. All the time she looked down at the street where she used to walk with her owner. The dog refused to eat and hardly drank.

On the seventh day, as the funeral procession of Jean Ricard was passing by on the way to the cemetery, the dog suddenly jumped from the balcony to commit suicide. It seemed as if the dog had waited for the whole week for this particular moment to plunge to her death. The mourners decided to open the coffin and put the faithful dog's body inside to reunite her with her master forever.

Eternal friendship

In the museum at Pompeii visitors can see two distorted figures side by side, a child and his dog. On the dog's collar is the following inscription in Latin: 'Thrice has this dog saved his little master from death, once from fire, once from flood, once from thieves.'

The dog actually chose to die with his little master when he realised that he could not save him. All the dogs in Pompeii except those tied up escaped from the city before the eruption of Vesuvius in 79 AD. This dog could have escaped like the others, but he chose to stay beside his master.

They are still beside each other more than nineteen hundred years later, and will remain so forever.

Chapter Nine

Dog friendships with other creatures

Canine teacher of the blind

One day last century near Lvov in Ukraine, a blind kitten was born. It seemed the poor kitten would have to be destroyed but to everybody's surprise, the kitten was helped by two farm dogs. From then on the kitten stopped blundering about and colliding with furniture. She was soon able to lead a fairly normal life as the dogs accompanied her on walks and protected her from attacks.

The dogs taught her to eat from their own plates and encouraged her in everything she tried to do. Thanks to their teaching and constant care, the once helpless kitten became a happy, confident and sociable cat despite her blindness.

Dog-hen friendship

A strange form of dog friendship with another creature was that between a dog and a hen. One such dog belonged to the British army of occupation in Germany. He was a fine cocker spaniel by the name of John. The dog used to roll on the hen. Although it appeared he would squash her, she seemed to enjoy the game. The hen in turn used to peck at the dog who also seemed to have fun.

In another case, a terrier called Rough used to share his meal with a hen. Every morning his owner ate a slice of bread spread with cream. The master shared his treat with the dog by breaking the corners of the slice and giving them to the dog. The dog always ate three of these pieces but he carried the fourth to a hen who each day waited for her canine friend. While the hen was eating the crust, the dog barked off any other hen who dared to try to participate in the feast.

Nipper's heroic feat

In April 1985 a fire broke out in a large barn on Austy Farm in Sussex (UK). The blaze spread so quickly that farm workers gave up their attempts to save the 300 animals trapped inside. But Nipper, the farm's five-year-old collie had a different view. He ran through the flames many times to rescue the terrified animals. Nipper ignored all the hardship and pain and continued his mission until all but nine animals were led out of the burning building.

During his incredible rescue mission Nipper was choked by fumes, his paws had blisters and his fur was burned in many places. For his heroic feat Nipper received the animal world's VC; a plaque with a dedication to the dog's intelligence and courage.

Chapter Ten

Dogs with bizarre interests

Most travelled US dog

Owney, a shaggy mongrel liked to travel by train. He always chose mail trains. Owney soon became a mascot for clerks in the US Post Office in Albany, New York. Realising the dog's unusual passion for train travel, the clerks decided to attach a special tag to his collar with a note in which they asked other Post Office clerks to stamp his collar so that a record could be kept of the dog's trips.

On 19 August 1895, Owney decided to travel overseas. He boarded a mail ship to Japan. His trip became such an international event that when he finally arrived in Japan, he was honoured by the Japanese emperor.

The famous traveller did not stop. His next destination was China. For the rest of his life Owney continued to travel around the world. When he died his body was exhibited in the Smithsonian Institution in Washington.

Chapter Eleven

Other strangest canine stories

Weird misunderstanding

A man lived along with his dog, a terrier, in a small house in a quiet street in Vienna. The man trained the dog to bring him each morning a packet of tobacco from the shop opposite. The dog was given a coin and the tobacconist knew what the dog required.

Some years later, the man moved to Prague. Naturally the man took his dog with him. In Prague, he expected the dog to continue bringing him tobacco as in Vienna. The man explained to the dog what he wanted him to do and notified a nearby tobacconist about his new canine customer. The dog seemed fully understood the man's instructions.

Time passed on the first day, and the dog did not return. The man became worried; he searched the city all day. But there was no sign of his dog.

Five days later, the man saw the dog carrying a packet of tobacco in front of the house. The dog was thin and almost too weak to stand. To his horror the man noticed that the packet had the wrapper of his former Vienna tobacconist. The dog wagged his tail and soon died from exhaustion. To bring tobacco to his master, the dog had run five days and four nights.

Strange haul

In the autumn of 1987, a fisherman's dog disappeared while swimming across a river in northern Siberia. Minutes later when the fisherman cast his net he hauled in a huge pike weighing 52 kg. He noticed with surprise a tail sticking out of the fish's jaws. The fisherman immediately cut the fish open and to his astonishment he saw his missing dog struggling out of his temporary prison. This event was reported in the Soviet press on 9 October 1987.

Dog TV

In 1985, in Prairie Village, a small town in Kansas, a special TV program was started exclusively for a dog audience. It was probably the most bizarre TV program ever devised; all the actors were dogs. The idea came to Mr Mike Milkovich who auditioned 150 dogs for the job. His own dog, Spot, had a leading role. A fashion show for dogs was a regular part of the program. Spot was dressed for the occasion, in T-shirt, jeans and tennis shoes. On the T-shirt, there was the inscription: 'The only thing between me and my jeans is my fleas.'

According to surveys of dog owners, their canine pets had shown keen interest in the program, barking and howling approval at the dog actors on the screen.

Strangest canine laws

In old Europe, if suspected of a crime, dogs were usually treated by the law as humans. Dressed in human clothing, they were tried officially in human courts, and represented by defence counsel (who almost always lost the case). It was even common to put an accused dog to the rack in an effort to extract a confession. The dog could then be put to death.

The weird law cropped up in a case in Austria. A

drummer's dog bit a member of a municipal council on the leg. The dog was sentenced by the court to a year's imprisonment in a narrenkottenlein. That is a kind of pillory or iron cage used for blasphemers or other criminals. The cage with the dog inside was then placed in the market square. As though he was a human prisoner, the poor dog was mocked and pelted with filth throughout the whole sentence.

According to the oldest surviving Digest of South German Law, dogs and other household animals were regarded as accessories to every crime committed by the householder and had to be punished like the humans. If the punishment for a person was beating, his animals were also beaten; if a man was burned for his crime so were his animals.

Trials of dogs have even occasionally been performed this century. In 1906, in Switzerland, a dog was tried and sentenced to death for taking part in a murder committed by a man. His human accomplice was, however, not sentenced to death but condemned to life imprisonment. Why the man was spared and the dog killed, remains a mystery.

Strangest canine laws of today

In Sweden it is illegal to castrate a dog.

Keeping dogs has been illegal in Iceland's capital, Reykjavik, since 1924. Keeping dogs is also illegal in the Maldives.

In China's capital, Beijing, ownership of dogs is banned, but city inhabitants can visit a special park where they can borrow a dog for a short while.

Blind pup's little pal

When two very beautiful Labrador cross pups were brought into an animal rescue centre in Devon, the centre's workers envied the dogs' future owners. The much admired canine babies were both eight-weeks old. One was black and one was brown. Soon, one of the workers noticed the brown puppy had no sense of direction. After careful examination it was found that the poor little fellow, despite his lovely soft eyes, was totally blind.

The blind puppy was not in a hopeless situation, however. The other puppy had discovered his problem before the humans did and he did everything to help his poor mate. During feeding, the black puppy always pushed him gently in the direction of his food bowl; the same happened at bedtime. Other times they played happily and the blind puppy enjoyed himself as much as the healthy puppy. No one seeing them playing would ever guess that one was blind.

The blind pup had extraordinary hearing, and he could always go immediately to a calling voice.

The puppies became TV celebrities, and a home was sought for them. The public responded enthusiastically to the appeal, evidently touched by the generosity of the black puppy.

Sadly, just a day before the pups were to go to their new owner the blind puppy died from the brain disease which it was believed had been the cause of his blindness.

From driver's cabin to royal palace

When British lorry driver, Tom Gillen, bought Kathy as a tiny puppy he did not believe she would grow into a very large dog. His friends warned him that she was of a large breed. But he ignored their advice. He was soon strongly attached to his pet, but eventually she became very big indeed. She was a Pyrenees mountain dog. She weighed nearly 60 kg, had a girth of 1 m and stood 75 cm high.

Tom continued to take his pet on all his trips. One day though he was laid off. Now he couldn't afford to feed her. He had no choice but to part with his beloved pet. So Tom left Kathy at an animal sanctuary in Kent. He told the carers that the dog could not be confined by any kennel or fence.

Kathy's next owners, however, disregarded the warnings and kept her in a kennel. She escaped easily. Kathy's next unfortunate owners had to return her after she smashed a window in the room where she was locked. Every time Kathy escaped she rushed to the motorway leading to Tom Gillen's house.

Kathy soon became famous. She was featured on the children's TV program Blue Peter. The program host explained the problems, particularly financial, which are associated with owning a large dog.

Kathy's plight was even described in the British press, leading to a dog miracle. Shortly after, the animal sanctuary received the following command on regal stationery: 'On no account have Kathy put to sleep. Put her on a flight from Heathrow addressed to: The Duchess of Alba, The Palace, Madrid.' The duchess saved the dog.

Kathy's new home is a 100-room castle in a twenty-five hectares garden. She settled down well with her new family and socialised successfully with the other royal dogs.

Blind leading the colour blind

In 1984, Kentucky brain surgeon, William Bowen's sight deteriorated so much that he had only peripheral vision. In other words, he could only distinguish shapes of objects. William was declared legally blind and he was provided with a trained guide dog which was called Sir Anheuser Bush II.

A couple of years later, William and his girlfriend were at a local night club where he got very drunk. While his girlfriend was driving William home, they had a quarrel about her driving. Eventually the angry girl stopped the car in the middle of the road, and walked off.

But William had total confidence in his own abilities, helped along by his intoxication. William slid over into the driving seat and ordered Deirdre the dog to leap on to the front seat next to him. William told his pet to bark once for a green traffic light, and twice for red. Confident that the dog would do as ordered, William drove off. He could not see the white lines dividing the road, but he was able to discern the light from street lamps, so he had a general idea where the road was.

But, the car weaved all over the road. Remember, that apart from being blind, William was blind drunk as well. Eventually William's poor driving was spotted by a traffic policeman. William was stopped and arrested for several serious traffic offences.

In court in Louisville, Kentucky, later that morning, William insisted that it was not him who had committed the offences, but his dog. Deirdre was driving, not William. He admitted that dogs are colour blind and cannot distinguish between red and green different traffic lights. But William insisted that his dog could discern different lights by their location on the pole.

Half way through the proceedings though, William changed his plea to guilty. He confessed that he felt horribly at fault, but not because of the traffic hazard he had caused. He felt bad for having unjustly blamed his beloved pet.

Sewing by dog power

In the 1870s, some French households used dog-driven sewing machines. The machine had a special set of wheels which could be worked by a small dog. The dog had to run round and round a movable disc, the same way as horses turn water wheels. The use of the sewing machines was eventually banned after protests by the French Society for Prevention of Cruelty to Animals.

Fire dog

One day in 1882, a stray mongrel sniffed at the hoofs of a horse at the London horse-omnibus station and greeted.him with a bark. The horse, Bruce, reacted by shaking his head and neighing. And so, a great friendship was born. The dog settled in at the station, greeting his horse friend each morning, and then in the evening after Bruce returned from work.

One day a fire broke out in a nearby building off Fleet Street. A horse-drawn fire engine arrived to put it out. Firefighter Dick Tozer had just rescued a man from the fire when suddenly, as if from nowhere, the mongrel appeared. He was barking frantically and making runs towards the doorway of the burning building. Dick realised the dog was telling him someone still remained inside.

Following the dog in, Dick came to a locked door which the dog scratched at excitedly. The fireman smashed the door and rushed into the room. There, a young girl lay, overcome by fumes. Dick grabbed her and carried her outside.

The clever little dog was adopted by the Chandos Street Fire Station. He was called Chance, and he was given a collar with the following inscription: 'Stop me not, but onward let me jog, for I am Chance, the London fireman's dog.'

Chance was a perfect fireman. He was able to get through the smoke faster than any human. He could find an injured person inside the building when nobody else could. And he actually invented his own method of entering a burning house. He would break a window with the hind part of his body and enter the room backwards.

Some months later, the station bought new horses. One of them was Bruce, Chance's friend from the horse-omnibus station. Witnesses of their reunion reported that the dog began to run around in delight while the horse tossed his head and pawed the ground.

But when Bruce was called to his first fire, he became mad with fear. When he smelt the smoke he began to rear on his hind legs. He had to be unhitched from the fire cart. Immediately he was free, he bolted. Chance ran to help. He barked loudly at Bruce, and the horse must have understood the dog's message as be began to slow down. Chance seized the end of the trailing rein in his teeth, dragged the horse's head around, and led him back.

Generous well wishers

When Norihiko Nishiyama of Osaka in Japan, advertised in the local paper to find his missing dog, he did not expect the readers' response. His dog was never found, but many readers felt sorry for him and offered him dogs. The man and his wife fell in love with all the new pets and kept them.

Soon though, neighbours began complaining about the unbearable noise. Norihiko Nishiyama would not even contemplate parting with any of his new dogs. Instead he opted to move away from his neighbours. He built a new isolated house in the mountains and now lives there happily with his multitude of pets.

Dog saves bird

Young Nick Conner and his collie Chip, were playing on the beach near their Sussex home. The boy was throwing his ball as far out to sea as he could and the dog was fetching it. Suddenly, instead of fetching the ball Chip swam a further 200 metres out to sea. He was swimming towards a small creature struggling helplessly in the water. Nick saw the dog examine the creature briefly and then swim back to shore with the animal in his mouth. It turned out to be a seagull so tangled in a fishing line that it was unable to fly. While Nick was trying to free the bird, the dog watched carefully, he barked with joy when the bird was eventually freed and flew away.

Dog snarls up traffic

Ringo, an orphan part St Bernard was adopted by the Saleh family of West Virginia. He quickly became attached to two-and-a-half-year-old Randy Saleh. Randy liked to run away from home but was always accompanied by Ringo.

One day, the tiny boy and his dog were found not far from home where traffic was banked up on a busy street. Forty cars were jammed there. The street was being terrorised by a 'mad' dog. The dog was Ringo. He was carefully guarding Randy who was playing in the middle of the traffic.

If one of the banked up cars attempted to move forward, Ringo leapt at it barking angrily and snarling. Every few minutes the dog would leave his post and try to gently push Randy to the side of the road. But to the small boy it was a game. Every time he rushed back to the middle of the roadway, to resume playing, and laughing.

Eventually a passer-by managed to take Randy away to the side of the street. The exhausted dog immediately left his post, realising that his little master was safe. Ringo became famous for his feat, and later was awarded the Ken-L-Ration Gold Medal as Dog Hero of the Year.

Chapter Twelve

Strangest-looking cats

Cats with two of this or that

Door-to-door salesman Dan Lizza was astonished one day to find his female cat giving birth to a two-faced kitten. At first he thought he was seeing double.

The strange-looking kitten was born in Latrobe, Pennsylvania, USA. The cat was given the name Gemini, the twins star sign. The other three kittens in the litter were normal.

In 1978 a cat with four ears was born in Chattanooga, Tennessee.

There are several reported cases of cats born with double tails.

Racoon-like cats

There is a breed of cat with fur which looks like a racoon's coat. This cat breed is called marine coon and it is a hybrid. It was probably originally a cross between an Angora (or some other long-tail breed) and an American shorthair cat. People used to be convinced that the creature was a hybrid of the domestic cat and the racoon. In fact, a woman even wrote to the pet column of an American newspaper asking for guidance in arranging mating between the two animals.

She did not realise that animals belonging to different families cannot interbreed.

Rabbit-cats

Some people still believe in the existence of a creature they call a cabbit — a cross between a cat and a rabbit. These people even claim to have seen such a creature. What they have actually seen is a tailless Manx-type cat which has long back legs and a rabbit-like hopping gait. This ignorance about cat breeds has led to enormous newspaper headlines, and in 1977 such a cat was exhibited in Los Angeles as a cabbit.

Strangest cat breed

The strangest breed of cat is the sphynx or Canadian hairless. It is the only breed of cat that sweats and for this reason it has to be sponged periodically.

The Aztecs had hairless cats. These are now extinct, but they were found in Mexico as recently as the late nineteenth century. In 1902, a sheep farmer in New Mexico was the owner of the last two examples, which he had bought from some local Indians.

Chapter Thirteen

Cats with incredible abilities

Flying cats

In June 1966 a flying black cat terrorised the community of Alfred, Ontario, Canada. Jean J. Revers, a confectioner there, noted 'it took gliding jumps of fifty or sixty feet. Wings extended after a good running start.' Revers claimed that the creature was able to remain about a foot above the ground. When the flying cat attacked his neighbour, Revers fired five bullets into the strange animal and killed it.

Policeman Terence Argyll who examined the cat's body found that 'its head resembled a cat's, but a pair of needle-sharp fangs, five-eighths of an inch long protruded from the mouth. It had a cat's whiskers, tail and ears, and its eyes were dark greenish and glossy.' The bizarre cat had a wing span of 36 cm and it weighed about 5 kg.

This was not the only flying cat reported in Canada in 1966. Another flying feline was shot near Lachute, a village near Montreal. And in June 1966, three black flying cats were reported in villages in Ontario and near Montreal.

Cat's power of thought

In an interesting experiment in 1970, Dr Helmut Schmidt placed a cat in a garden shed. Warmth for the cat was from a

200 watt electric lamp connected to a generator. Positive and negative pulses periodically turned the generator on and off. Normally, the generator and lamp were on about half of the time.

Dr Schmidt found that whenever the cat was inside the shed the generator turned more positive pulses so was turned on for longer periods than it should have been. Thus the cat received more warmth than he should have.

When the cat was not in the shed, the generator worked absolutely normally. Dr Schmidt calculated the odds against the results being mere chance, as about 60 to 1.

Cat conspires with a ghost

An old sailor from Istanbul tells the story of a Liberian ship with a cat on board and the ghost of a murdered man.

The death occurred on the ship during a brawl. Two drunk sailors started fighting. One of them pushed the other so that his head struck a steel bulkhead and fractured his skull. He died on the spot. The dead man had only one close friend, a Siamese cat.

Soon after the murder, his cat began to act very strangely. He behaved as if his master was still alive. The cat woke up precisely at the time his owner would, then at the usual time went to the washroom, and to the saloon and so on as if the sailor were still alive. The crew believed that the cat was following the dead man's ghost.

Soon, perhaps with the help of his deceased master's ghost, the cat had his revenge by killing the man who caused his master's death. The cat apparently got into the cabin while the man was sound asleep and drunk, and curled up over his mouth and nose, to suffocate him.

The cat had not seen the fight between the two sailors so there was no way he could know by conventional means who had killed his master. Nor was there any way of entering the killer's cabin by conventional means because the door had been locked from the inside. There was a spare key, but the cat's dead owner knew where it was. Crew members speculated that the ghost of the cat's master opened the door to help the cat to take revenge.

Cats with gift of the gab

A woman in Toulon, France claimed that her cat could talk and that she often asked her for advice. The cat's advice, she claimed was full of wisdom and she always followed it. When the remarkable cat died she decided to give her a 'decent' burial. Cats may not be buried in a church yard so she buried her against the wall of her local church tower.

In 1948, Vincent Quintana, a Spaniard from Santander, and twenty-nine other people swore that they heard a local cat say in Spanish 'Let met alone. Shut up.'

In a mansion in Ireland, an angry butler threw a potato at his cat, hitting it in the face. The offended cat responded with a prolonged blood curdling yowl. Then everyone heard the cat actually uttering words which were clearly addressed to his assailant. The cat said; 'I was here before you, and I'll still be here when you've gone!' Next day the butler was dead.

Cats predict disasters

During World War II, people being evacuated to Exeter were astonished to see dozens of cats walking out into the countryside in the direction of Tiverton. The purpose of the cats' sudden march became clear when later that night there was a devastating air raid on Exeter.

Two cats, pets on the destroyer HMS *Salmon*, had never shown any inclination to leave the ship. On the morning before its disastrous last voyage, the two cats tried hard to leave the ship. The cats' first attempts failed, but just as the ship was weighing anchor the two leapt to another ship which was just tying up alongside. Later the same day the entire crew of the *Salmon* perished as their ship was torpedoed and sank.

Cats predict earthquake

Just before the 1908 earthquake in Messina, an inhabitant of that city saw his cats scratching at the door of the room. They seemed greatly excited and very frightened. When he let them out of the room, they ran downstairs and started to scratch even more violently at the door leading to the street.

Perplexed by their unusual behaviour, he opened the door and followed his pets until they reached the edge of the city. Even in the countryside the cats seemed to be terrified as they scratched and tore at the grass. Soon the man understood why. An earthquake struck and all the houses in the city were demolished.

Cat predicts TV explosion

In a village in southern Poland a cat named Macius liked his owner's television set, not for its telecasts, but as a warm place to sleep. The family watched TV for hours, and the cat stayed there until the set was switched off.

One night, however, as the family watched, Macius woke up, leapt to the floor, and raced out the door. Minutes later there was a shattering 'bang'. The TV tube disintegrated and the whole room was showered with glass like shrapnel. In his normal place on the TV, the cat would certainly have been wounded or even killed by the explosion.

Cats forecast weather

A Kansas farmer recounts that his cat could predict a tornado and even know which buildings would be destroyed. His cat was mother of four kittens. She lived with them in a barn close to his farmhouse. One day, the farmer noticed that one of the kittens had disappeared; hours later a second one had gone and then the third, and finally the whole feline family had gone missing.

On the very night the mother and her kittens vanished, a tornado struck, completely destroying the barn.

Next morning, farmers in another area noticed four kittens and the mother cat in their own barn, miles away from where the tornado had struck. Somehow, the cat knew when and where the tornado would strike and carried her babies to safety.

Swimming cats

Few people know that one breed of cat loves to swim. The breed originated in the region around Lake Van in Turkey and are known as Vancats. They love water and they begin to swim early in life. When there is no other opportunity Vancats will even swim in a bathtub.

Even in other breeds a cat which loves to swim can be found occasionally. *Pearson's Weekly* reported in 1896: 'A lady living near the Thames has a cat which frequently swims across the river to a spot which is infested with rats. Pussy always swims very low in the water with tail erect, and shakes herself like a dog on coming ashore.'

In April 1945, *Country Life* published photographs of a swimming cat. The water-loving cat was called Tony and belonged to Ms Alice Marshall. According to Ms Marshall 'Tony was very fond of going on the river in a punt and always chose the same spot for a swim, purring with pleasure in anticipation as he neared the spot. He walked down the paddle from the punt and swam off tail up to the opposite bank.'

Cunning hunter

A cat in Collander in Wyoming, was a very clever hunter of rats. One day, he was seen to take a piece of beef and go to a rat-hole. He put the piece of beef by the side of the rat-hole and hid nearby. When the rat appeared the cat sprang up and killed it.

Most intelligent cat

Peri-Nympsie, a Siamese cat owned by Miss Leonie Norris in Worcestershire, UK, was regarded as perhaps the most intelligent of all the cats in the world. This unique female cat was born in 1927.

She was said to be able to understand a vocabulary of more than 200 words. Peri-Nympsie understood so much of what Leonie was saying that when she said 'You are so sympathetic, Peri-Nympsie', the cat always kissed her in response.

The cat even tried to help her owner to dust and sweep floors. In fact, Leonie said 'I made her a little apron and tied it around her neck whenever she felt domesticated.' According to her owner, the cat even pretended to help in the preparation of dinner. Peri-Nympsie once saved her owner from a burglar. When he entered the cottage the cat jumped off the mantelpiece and attacked the intruder so ferociously that he became frightened and ran away.

The cat genius died in 1932. *Fur and Feather* magazine printed an obituary, describing her as 'Human in her intelligence, fierce in her loyalty and lastingly remembered in love, pride and gratitude'.

Cat super navigators

Scientists have long been fascinated and perplexed by the ability of cats to travel long distances through unknown territory to a specific destination. There are so many well confirmed cases that they cannot be dismissed as mere luck.

When an army sergeant in Kokomo, Indiana was transferred to a base in Augusta, Georgia he took his cat with him. The cat did not like his new destination though, and he made the 1120 km trip back to his previous home. The cat somehow managed to cover this very long distance in only three weeks. The cat did not simply remember the route back to Indiana. He had travelled to Georgia with his owner in an express train.

A fascinating experiment to examine this mysterious ability of cats was performed by Presch and Lindenbaum in Germany. They put a number of cats into separate boxes and took them several miles from their homes and then released them in a labyrinth containing twenty-four exits. Eighty per cent of the cats emerged from the exits that faced in the direction of their own homes. If it was just a result of simple luck, the success rate would have been about eight in two hundred.

Some people believe that the cats may be scent-trailing. Some cats, however, took such a long time to return home that it is unlikely that scent traces could have lasted that long. One cat, for instance, was lost in Maine-et-Loire, France, where his owner had taken him during the family holiday. This cat returned home after ten months absence and travelled a distance of 740 km.

Feline music critics

Some cats are very sensitive to music, and some singers or composers highly value their cat's opinion. Theophile Gautier, the poet, had a cat called Madame who was a typical feline music critic: 'sitting on a pile of scores she listened attentively and with visible signs of pleasure to singers. But piercing notes made her nervous and at the high A, she never failed to close the mouth of the singer with her soft paw. This was an experiment which it amused many to make and which never failed. It was impossible to deceive this cat dilettante on the note in question . . .'

Mademoiselle Dympny, a great harpist of the seventeenth century, used to say that she owed her success to her cat. When she was playing she constantly looked for her cat's signs of pleasure or displeasure. The cat provided feedback and hence helped her to improve her playing.

Paderewski the Polish pianist and composer also highly valued the 'opinion' of cats. When he was a young man, and making his debut at St James's in London, he was disappointed to see only about a hundred people sitting in the hall. Nervously, Paderewski turned to the hall cat and whispered in his ear 'Wish me luck'. The cat responded by jumping on his lap and purring. The performance was a great success and the delighted pianist later honoured the cat too by playing especially for him the 'Cat's Fugue' in the artists' Green Room. He claimed that this composition was suggested to him by his own cat walking up the keyboard.

Feline snake hunters

In Paraguay cats are employed in hunting snakes, especially rattlesnakes. The cats are trained in a strategy to help hunters to overpower the deadly snake. The cat strikes the snake with its paw and slips to one side to avoid a counterattack. As the snake lunges, the hunter catches it behind the head.

Cat bearing gifts

This rather sentimental story comes from long ago when public transport still relied on horses. A cat lived in a shop next to a horse-omnibus depot. One day, a new kitten was brought to the shop and the cat showed his anger by moving out. He settled in across the yard.

However, the attitude of the older cat soon changed dramatically.

His dislike of the kitten ceased, and he did everything he could to help the kitten. There had been a sad accident. A horse trod on one of the kitten's paws. The poor little kitten received medical help, and the paw was bandaged. The older cat made every effort to help the suffering kitten. He caught mice and offered one every day to his new friend.

Fortunately, the kitten's disability was not very serious and she soon recovered.

Feline computer crime

Morris, a Siamese cat, while dancing on his owner's personal computer in San Francisco, accidentally pressed a secret five-letter code that accessed a business memory bank and erased $100,000 worth of account files. The company subsequently had to re-program their entire computer system.

Most eccentric cat

In Buenos Aires in 1948 a black female cat called Mincho ran up a 12 m tree, and never came down again.

This eccentric cat survived because of the generosity of local people who were fond of the stubborn cat. They used to push food and milk up to her on a long pole. It was her only source of food. The strange cat sat on the treetop for more than six years; during her self-imposed exile in the tree however, she managed to produce three litters of kittens.

Galloping cats

Cat-racing has a long tradition. In 1936, a cat-racing track was built in Portisham in Dorset, UK. The course was about 200 m long and the feline runners were chasing a moving electric mouse. Their maximum speed was half that of greyhounds.

The races were organised by the management of the local pub, and were a great success. About fifty cats took part in the first two race meetings and attracted some 500 people. The cat athletes were trained for the races. The best performers were cats less than three years old.

Puss climbing champions

One of the greatest cat climbers was chased by a savage dog, and climbed 21.3 m up the sheer wall of a block of flats at Laisterdyke, Yorkshire, UK and hid in a gap just below the roof. The cat was later rescued by an RSPCA officer. The cat accomplished his feat only because the building had been pebble-dashed, and provided a gripping surface.

A ginger tom ended up on top of a 45 m chimney stack at Wolfenden mill in Botton, near Manchester and stayed there for nearly 30 hours before he was rescued. The cat had climbed up a ladder while the chimney was being repaired.

The greatest feline mountaineer was a female cat who walked to Kandersteg in 1928 and established her home in the Blumlisalp Club hut at the height of 2734 m. She was adopted by a hut guardian. One day the cat of her own free will decided to accompany some climbers to the summit. She became fond of mountain climbing and reached Blumlisalphorn (3668 m) in the Swiss Alps a number of times.

Even more incredible is the four-month-old kitten who in September 1950 followed her owner Josephine Aufdenblatten and other climbers to the top of the 4505 m Matterhorn in Switzerland. She was rewarded with a share of their food.

Cats dancing

One night in Paris, Madame Pauline Michelet was having dinner in a house facing the Café Turc where a ball was taking place. She claimed later that on the roof of the house opposite, above the restaurant, she counted nine cats moving calmly to the music, backs arched, paws rising and falling. When the band finished playing the waltz and began playing a quadrille, the cats began to leap about as if they were crazy.

Cat artist

The artistic career of Topsy the cat of Dr George Cooper, of Hertford began when she became interested in pencils and crayons which had been left around the house by the doctor.

One day Dr Cooper had an idea; he suspended a pencil from a piece of string in front of a sheet of paper. At first the cat only played with the pencil as if it was a toy. Suddenly, however, she took the pencil in her paw and started to draw lines on the paper.

'I had read of a chimpanzee in America painting a picture, so I thought, why can't a cat do it?' Dr Cooper said. 'When I looked at the results the outline was there and all I did was darken some of the lines and give one picture a wash.'

The talented cat drew six pictures for an exhibition held in Foyle's Gallery in London. Sketches by the cat were hung alongside the paintings of her owner. Only Dr Cooper's pictures were for sale. He refused to sell his talented cat's pictures.

Chapter Fourteen

Feline doctors

Cat healers

Cats sometimes play quite an important role in therapy for mentally and physically ill people. Cats can be found in hospitals, schools for the handicapped, alcohol and drug addiction units and old people's homes. As Professor Samuel Corson of Ohio State University explains. 'Seriously ill people who play with cats and other pets become different people; they receive the kind of love which helps the most.'

In 1991, researchers at Cambridge University found out that just months after purchasing a cat or dog, people suffer less from such common health problems as flu, backache and headache.

In 1992 it was reported that Australians who own pets tend to have less cholesterol in their blood than people without pets having similar lifestyles. Pet ownership may reduce the chances of developing a serious heart disease.

Egyptian feline doctor

Bastet was the cat goddess of sun, moon and motherhood. She was responsible, among other things, for the success of crops, rain making and protection of the dead.

When a child of a wealthy man was sick, the parents

sought the help of the feline goddess. The relatives of the sick child shaved all the hair off their heads and sold it for gold or silver. The money was then given to the guardians of the temple to buy milk and fish for the temple cats that were worshipped there.

The family then assembled in the temple and the cats began eating the food while the priests chanted. The family watched the eyes of the cats to find out whether their beloved child would recover or not.

Cats in Chinese medicine

In remote parts of China bronchitis is treated by mixing powdered cat's skull with alcohol. Charred, powdered cat skull mixed with oil was the remedy for rabies. Deep running sores can be cured by eating a soup of cat flesh.

Cats in Japanese medicine

The truly incredible Japanese remedy for gastritis and epilepsy is to put a live, black cat on the patient's stomach and keep it there for three or four hours.

Healing cats of Europe

In the Roman Empire cats were used in medicinal treatments and cures. Pliny (AD 61 - 113) claimed that cat's dung would cure various diseases. Mixed with wine from a thick paste, cat dung was used to draw thorns out from the flesh. Mixed with mustard it was an excellent poultice for drawing ulcers of the head. But to cure uterine ulcers the dung had to be mixed with oil of roses and swallowed.

Various parts of the cat's body were employed to cure ailments. In 1607, it was reported that bladder stones could be cured by medicine made from powdered cat's liver.

More complicated was a remedy for failing eyesight.

A black cat had to be killed and its head burnt to a cinder and ground to a fine powder.

This powder then had to be blown gently into the eyes with a quill.

Even cat's fur was considered to have medicinal value. It was a common remedy for burns. In fact, many cats were killed and skinned for this purpose, especially after the Great Fire of 1666 in London. The cats fur was laid over the badly burned areas of the body.

Probably the most medicinally important part of the cat's anatomy was its tail. Even recently, in some country areas of England, it was believed that irritation caused by stye can be relieved by simple rubbing the affected eyelid with the tail of a black cat.

In Cornwall, this treatment was accompanied by a spell; 'I poke thee, O, qualy way, O qualy way.' In the county of Northamptonshire, the swollen eyelid was cured by stroking it with a hair pulled from the tip of the tail of a black cat. The hair had to be plucked on the night of a new moon and drawn nine times across the stye.

Feline miracle worker

A Boston family had only one child, a boy called Bobby. He was a handsome, intelligent and happy child. All this began suddenly changing however as the boy entered his teenage years. He began to experience visions and to suffer from depression. He was soon unable to cope at school and gradually all his friends deserted him. It seemed as if the boy was being controlled by some mysterious evil forces. The best psychiatric help achieved nothing. The boy's condition continued to regress. When he was fourteen, Bobby was no longer able to feed himself. Finally, he stopped talking and after three months his eye movement ceased and he had no facial expression.

After six months of silence it seemed Bobby would never recover. One day the family noticed that he moved his eyes whenever he was shown a picture of a cat. Someone came up with an idea; perhaps the boy would respond even better to a live cat. A live kitten was brought and placed on his lap. Bobby immediately reacted by moving his head forward and looking down at the friendly pet. Several minutes later the boy made his first voluntary action for months. He raised his hand and began to pat the kitten. After about an hour Bobby began talking to the cat; although his speech was monosyllabic it was a gigantic step forward. After about two and a half months of the daily contact with the kitten Bobby's condition improved so dramatically that he was able to talk to his doctor.

Bobby's progress continued and his dramatic recovery looked like a miracle. He soon went back to school. The cat who brought his recovery became his closest friend.

Chapter Fifteen

Feline detectives and policemen

Cat solves murder mystery

Poona the cat solved the mystery murder of Peggy Pease in India. Peggy loved animals and when her husband, a veterinary surgeon retired, they opened a small animal hospital, where they helped every animal they could. After her husband's death, Peggy continued the good work until well into her seventies. But health problems forced her to close down the sanctuary. Despite being ill, however, she continued to look after stray animals including several cats, one of whom was Poona.

The old lady had three servants, a young boy, a cook who was almost as old as herself and a middle-aged man. Now suffering from ill-health Peggy rarely left home. So when she disappeared nobody noticed her absence. When two friends came to see her, they were surprised that neither Peggy nor her servants were at home. The visitors immediately called the police who were themselves unable to find the missing quartet. The detectives only found four cats locked in a windowless cupboard. Three of the cats were so weak that they soon died. Poona somehow survived.

Poona then visited the police station every day. The murder mystery was still unresolved. Then one of the detectives had an idea; he took Poona back to her missing owner's home. There he gave the cat an item of Peggy's clothing. The idea was that the cat may be able to follow a human scent like a dog. For several minutes the cat remained motionless. Then he walked to a nearby patch of tangled vegetation and stopped. The investigating officer searched the bushes and found a wooden mallet stained with blood and hair.

Now Poona began to search for the body of her missing owner. First, the cat began to stare at the house without moving. Then suddenly, she walked slowly towards a flower bed and began scratching vigorously at the earth. The policemen dug and soon discovered the body of the old lady and her cook.

The boy and Peggy's middle-aged servant still could not be found. The police discovered the whereabouts of the middle-aged servant and interrogated him. He explained his absence from the house by saying that Ms Pease gave him permission to visit his sick brother. His fingerprints had been found on the mallet, but he said that he used it when doing various odd jobs around the house.

It appeared there would be no progress in the case and the subject could not be convicted for lack of evidence. The officer decided to bring in Poona to see her reaction. When the cat saw the suspect she immediately flew for the man's face, spitting and clawing ferociously. When the detective explained to him how the cat had found both the murder weapon and the victims' bodies, the accused man was terrified. The illiterate servant concluded immediately that Poona must have magical power. He knew that the lady's cats had not witnessed the burial or the murder weapon used. So he confessed. He said he had been so enraged by Ms Pease's decision to dismiss him when she caught him stealing, that he returned to her house and killed her. To eliminate witnesses, he also killed the two servants. He had thrown the boy's body into a river.

Feline martial arts master

One night, two hold-up men burst into Abbots Morton sub-post office and began cutting into the wire screen around the counter. The noise woke the office cat, Lucky, who was dozing on his favourite chair. Unlike the terrified postmistress who retreated, the cat was not afraid of the criminals. He leaped on the back of one and, hissing furiously, dug in his claws. His victim began screaming in pain, and the other criminal became frightened. They both ran off empty-handed.

The brave cat was awarded a certificate of merit by the postal authorities. The cat was also given a special gourmet chicken dinner.

Chapter Sixteen

Ghost and monster cats

Evil feline ghost

A very aggressive cat called Scree fought everything that dared to come near him. When Scree died in 1946 and was buried in his owner's garden in Aldwick, Sussex, it appeared that peace would return to the neighbourhood. Nothing could have been further from the truth. One evening, soon after, the woman heard a weird, half-human cry from her garden. She opened the back door and horrified she saw the ghost of the dead cat standing on his own grave. Soon afterwards, the local paper, the *Bognor Post* began following the cat-ghost story: 'Scree exerted his wicked dictatorship more than ever before. His owner acquired another cat. It died mysteriously. She got another. This one died. Two other cats in the vicinity were found with their throats slashed. They had to be put to sleep.'

A neighbour saw Scree attacking her own cat. The neighbour's cat was found mauled and dying. Blood and fur were strewn all over the garden.

Feline ghost detector

Robert Morris of Duke University went to investigate a haunted house in Kentucky, taking with him four animal ghost-detectors. One was a cat.

Each animal was taken in turn to the room where a murder had been committed. Just after entering the room, the dog began to snarl and then refused to stay. No one could persuade it to re-enter the room, even with food rewards. The rat behaved normally. The cat at first behaved like the dog. When it reached the same spot as the dog, it leaped up on its owner's shoulders. Later the cat jumped to the floor, and began spitting and hissing while staring at the empty chair. The rattlesnake also appeared to perceive the ghost, since it coiled itself into attack posture while focusing on the same unoccupied chair.

Human sacrifice for monster cats

According to Japanese legend, a village was once so terrorised by supernatural cats that feline monsters were given a virgin girl sacrifice once a year. The virgin girl was selected each year by drawing lots. She was tied in a special cage and left for the monster cats to devour.

A travelling warrior who learned about the barbaric custom decided to do something to stop it. One year, he asked the chosen girl's parents not to place her inside the cage. In a dream the warrior learned that the monster cats were terrified of a certain dog. He borrowed the dog from its owner and the dog was placed in the cage instead of the girl.

When the monster cats entered the cage the dog leapt out and attacked them. The warrior who was waiting behind the cage decapitated one monster cat, and the others ran away terrified, and never came back.

Chapter Seventeen

Horror stories about cats

Exploding cat

For eight years, a cat named Peppi lived happily in Anmer Lodge, a home for old people, in Stanmore in London. One day Peppi was lying in a chair in the day lounge, having his usual nap. Suddenly, there was a huge bang and a flash and the cat flew several feet into the air. During the explosion he was enveloped in a sheet of blue flame. Firemen who were called to investigate the phenomenon blamed it on a build-up of static electricity which had accumulated on Peppi's fur.

Feline eyewitness

When a woman was murdered in Lyon, in France the assassins did not worry about the cat which witnessed the murder. The oversight cost them their lives.

When the police came, they saw a large white cat sitting on a table. The cat was sitting motionless, his eyes fixed on the body of his master, his look one of horror.

Next day, the cat was still sitting on the table. So many people in the room did not seem to frighten him. However, when the suspects were brought in, the cat's behaviour changed. His eyes glared with fury, and his hair bristled. He darted into the middle of the room where he stopped for a moment to stare at the suspects. For the first time, the faces of the assassins showed signs of guilt. Afterwards, they were brought to trial and condemned. Before their execution, they confessed.

Chapter Eighteen

Cats in rituals, magic and beliefs

Cats can bring corpses to life

Once, when someone died in China, the family immediately tied up all their cats or quickly moved them to the neighbours. The cats stayed tied or outside the property until the corpse was in its coffin. This precaution was taken because of the belief the cats have so-called 'soul-recalling hair'. If the cat that possesses such hair leapt or walked over a death bed, the body would rise up. The corpse would grasp somebody who would then die a horrible death.

To avoid this, the corpse had to be immediately offered something else to seize such as a broom handle, pole or piece of furniture. The corpse would then become very irate and grasp the object against its chest to cool its anger. Most times the corpse would soon calm down again.

Cat of Corpus Christi

In parts of France cats were so highly respected that they were sometimes involved in important religious ceremonies. At Aix-en-Provence, until late in the nineteenth century, on the feast of Corpus Christi, the most beautiful male cat was wrapped like a child in swaddling clothes. He was then carried through the streets, inside a richly decorated shrine.

As he passed, the waiting crowd bent their knees in reverence and dropped flowers on the ground before him. The cat was treated in all respects as the god of the day.

Pyre for pussies

At the festival of St John, in parts of France cats were treated barbarically. They were put into a basket and thrown into the middle of a great fire. The pyre in the public square was lit by the bishop and his clergy. Hymns and anthems were sung, and processions by the priest and people were made in honour of the sacrifice.

In Vosges, cats were traditionally burned alive on Shrove Tuesday because they were believed to be companions of the Devil. In Alsace, cats were immolated every Easter Sunday. In Paris, on the Place de Grève, baskets and sacks filled with cats were set afire as a part of mid-summer celebration. In 1648, King Louis XIV himself lit the fire and danced around the pyre while cats screamed in agony.

Feline goddess of sex

The ancient Egyptian goddess Bastet was the symbol of sexuality and fertility. She was depicted as a human with the head of a cat. The centre for cat worship was the city of Bubastis situated on the east of the Nile Delta.

During the annual festival in honour of Bastet 700,000 pilgrims travelled to that city. During the festival the Bastet temple's priests and worshippers imitated the mewing of their feline goddess.

Historians describe the festival as a drunken sexual orgy. According to Jean Cawtin: 'There is some evidence that the festival started while the participants were still travelling towards Bubastis in their boats. As they approached each city along the way, the boats would pull into the banks. The women would scream off-colour jokes and lewd suggestions at the gathering crowd, finally flinging their dresses up over their heads.

'This was repeated at every city and was a sign for those on shore who were unable to make the trip, to start their own sexual orgy at home.

'The sexual orgies were approved by the authorities, as it was strongly believed they would increase fertility of crops, women and animals.'

Sacred cat dishes

In ancient Egypt cats were considered divine. The family cat was often bedecked with jewels and ate from the same dish as its owner. The killing of a cat was an offence punishable by death. When an Egyptian saw a dead cat he lamented aloud with grief, beating his breast, irrespective of who owned the cat.

When a family cat died its owners displayed their grief by shaving off their eyebrows. Their funeral ceremonies depended on the importance of the cat. Temple cats were the most respected felines, and were laid to rest in true sarcophagi or tombs. Milk was put in their sacred vault and incantations of the temple priests were said to keep the sacred cat dishes eternally filled.

A cemetery of embalmed cats was discovered in Egypt in the middle of the nineteenth century. In it there were over 300,000 cat mummies. The mummified bodies, weighing a total of twenty tonnes, were shipped to Lancashire and sold to farmers there as fertiliser.

Japanese cult of the cat

In the modern world, the cat is most highly venerated in Japan. In Tokyo cats even have their own temple: Gotokuji. Cats in Japan are highly venerated after their death, and the cat temple is both their cemetery and a place of worship. The temple is built in typical Japanese style and is made of wood. The temple priests wear sacred vestments and intone religious chants for the repose of cat souls. Visitors pass two stone guardians of duty on entering the temple. These are to remind visitors that the death of a cat is as important as that of a human being and that appropriate reverence is demanded.

On the temple altar hundreds of cat images crowd against each other. They are sculptured, painted or carved relief. Each cat image has its right paw upraised to the height of its eyes as if to greet the visitor or attract his attention.

Japanese represent thus Maneki-Neko, the small female cat who is believed to bring happiness and good luck.

Buddhists of Tokyo bury their cats in this temple or nearby and on the same day offer a sculpture or painting resembling their cat at the temple altar. It is believed that this homage to fidelity will ensure the donor good luck in all their lifetime.

The cat cemetery is spread around the altar. Each grave is covered with tablets inscribed with prayers for the souls of the cats, with an image of Buddha in the corner of each.

At the temple doors all kinds of images of cat-sculptured in stone, hardwood or black marble are sold. People buy an image which closely resembles that of their deceased cat. Wealthier cat owners commission an appropriate statue during the lifetime of their beloved pet.

Women who turn into cats

During the infamous witchcraft trials of Europe in the sixteenth and seventeenth century many accused women admitted they were able to transform themselves into cats. As one French witch explained they had to change into cats in order to be able to pass unseen through the night. They accomplished this by rubbing their body with a special ointment.

A Scottish witch said in 1662 that to change oneself into a cat a special spell was required. It had to be chanted three times over. To return to human form it was only necessary to chant another spell.

Members of a coven were also able to turn one another into cats. If a witch in cat form met a witch in human form, she would say: 'The devil speed thee and go thou with me.' Then, immediately, the other witch would assume cat form and the two witches would run off as cats.

In 1584 Jonathan Baldwin wrote that a witch could only change into a cat nine times. He explained that this is because the cat had nine lives and the cat would haunt anyone who took one of its nine lives and seek revenge. For this reason, it was said many witches had wounds inflicted on them by cats.

There are any number of stories about witches who become cats. In one story told in Strasbourg, in France, a man walking late at night was suddenly attacked by three enormous cats. He defended himself and was able to escape unhurt but he was sure he had wounded some of the attacking cats. Later, the man was accused of attacking and wounding three notorious local women. He heatedly denied the accusations, but was horrified to learn that medical examination of the accusing women had revealed that injuries they had were almost identical with those he had inflicted on the attacking cats.

In another case, a Scottish laird found one day that many rare bottles were missing from his wine cellar. Armed with a sword he went to the cellar to check. He was suddenly attacked by several black cats. In the fight which ensued, the laird was able to defend himself and severely mutilated one of the cats. The rest fled. The laird learned next day to his great surprise that one of the local women was found dying in her cottage with one leg cut off.

Worship of the cat as Satan

Members of a religious sect called Templers confessed under torture that they worshipped the Devil in the form of a black tomcat.

Members of another sect called Luciferans believed that the Devil had been expelled from heaven unjustly and that in the future he would be restored to his former position. They worshipped a black cat and sacrificed young children to please the Devil.

An eleventh-century movement called Waldensians claimed that the Devil appeared to them in the form of a cat.

Disciples of the Persian prophet Mani, called Manicheans, asserted that humans were of Satanic origin. They believed the powers of God and the Devil were equal. They considered it necessary to constantly appease the Devil. The Devil was said to prefer to appear in the form of cat.

Their religious ritual began with the disciples chanting the names of various demons until Satan appeared in the form of a black male cat. Then all the lights were extinguished and each man there seized the nearest woman and had sex with her.

If a child was born as a result of these orgies, eight days after the birth a large fire was lit and the infant was burned on it. The ashes were collected and eaten by those present in the belief that this would help them never to forsake their faith.

Lord killed by cat magic

In 1618 Margaret and Philip Flower were executed at Lincoln in the UK for causing the death of Lord Henry Moss, eldest son of the Earl of Rutland. They had obtained his right glove which they rubbed on the back of their imp called Rutterkin. The imp was in the form of a cat and lived with them in their house.

The glove was then submerged in boiling water, pricked with a knife and buried in a dung-hill. This was done in the belief that as the glove rotted so would the liver of Lord Henry. And, indeed, that is exactly how he died.

Cats and the King of Siam

It used to be the custom that when a male member of the Siam royal family passed away, one of his favourite cats was buried alive with him. The tomb was constructed with small holes pierced in the roof to make it possible for a persevering and clever cat to escape.

If the cat succeeded in his escape attempt it was assumed that the soul of the buried royal family member had already passed into the cat. After that, the cat was treated with appropriate honours.

Moggy clocks

Before clocks were invented, the Chinese used cats as time keepers. They had observed that the pupils of the cats' eyes become steadily narrower until noon when they were said to be like fine hairs in the midday sun.

After midday, the cat's pupils began to dilate steadily until sunset. So to find out the time they simply grabbed the nearest cat, and stared closely in its eyes.

Better than catching rats

Cats were introduced to Japan from China in about the tenth century AD. They were called 'the tiger who eats out of the hand'. The Japanese Emperor Ichigo (AD 986–1011) was very fond of cats. On the ninth day of the ninth month of the year 999, when kittens were born in his palace, the emperor was so delighted that he ordered royal servants to attend them and provide them with the most delicious food. Each kitten was given beautiful clothes.

The Emperor conferred the rank of the fifth lady of the court upon the mother, one of his favourite cats. He named her Myobo no Omoto, meaning 'lady-in-waiting'.

Cat charms

In ancient Egypt, when a newly-wed couple decided on the number of children they wished to have they purchased a cat amulet, engraved with the appropriate number of kittens. It was worn by the wife as jewellery or kept at home as an ornament. The cat amulet was used as a ritual object during prayers to Bastet, the cat-goddess, asking her for the desired number of children.

Cat charms were also worn in ancient Egypt to ensure prosperity, good health and long life.

Lucky cat charms are popular throughout the world. In parts of China, even live cats are regarded as lucky. The cats are kept confined by long thin chains, fixed to a leather collar. The uglier and older the cats, the greater the luck they will bring the owner. If the cat escapes, the chances of good fortune also disappear. Even today some Chinese cats are kept collared and chained.

It was also customary in China to employ live cats to protect precious silkworms from rats. If live cats were not available cat pictures were fixed on the walls of the silkworm sheds.

The Chinese also used to attach clay effigies of sitting cats with staring, baleful eyes to the eaves of their houses.

Even now, cat pictures can still occasionally be seen in China. Some Buddhists believe that dark-coloured cats bring gold to the house while light-coloured cats bring silver.

Devil cats of Japan

In Japan, devil and witch cats were believed to be easily identified because they had two tails or one tail split into two. It was said that devil and witch cats could take human form and some of them turned into vampires. In young cats the split tail was not apparent at first.

To prevent kittens from turning into demons, their tails were sometimes cut off. This created among the Japanese a preference for bobtailed cats since it was believed they could not become demons.

Building sacrifice

In England and Ireland, to ward off the devil and to ensure good fortune cats were used as a building sacrifice.

The idea of building sacrifice has an ancient tradition. Originally the walled-in victim was not a cat but a human.

Occasionally, when a very old building is being demolished, the body of a cat is discovered. It is usually found between the boards of the floors or in the roof. In 1950, for instance, when alterations were made to a house near the Tower of London a number of feline bodies were discovered between the floor joists of an upper room. The building had been erected in about 1700. The cats' bodies were well preserved because it was customary in older times to apply smoke or special chemicals to the cat's body before it was walled up.

Building sacrifices were also believed to protect the new house from vermin. A cat found in the walls of Hay Hall in the north of England, was placed in a standing position with its jaws open and claws extended, facing a small bird. It was evident that a special cavity for this purpose had been made when the hall was constructed in the fourteenth century.

In a sixteenth-century house in Southwark, another cat's body was discovered. It was entombed there together with two rats, one in the cat's mouth and the other in his forepaws.

Feline building sacrifice was practised in Britain at least until 1890. In that year it was reported that builders in Cornwall refused to complete building a house because the owner did not want a building sacrifice. She evidently disliked the idea of sacrificing a poor cat. Finally a compromise was reached, and instead of a cat a hare was sacrificed and the construction of the building was completed on time.

Thievish cats

In 1699, in the Swedish town of Mohra, about 300 children were taken to court accused of being witches. The prosecutor stated that: 'the Devil gave to each of them ... a young cat, its duty being to steal the butter, cheese, milk and bacon which they then offered to the Prince of Darkness. The thievish cats accompanied them to the palace of Satan, and shared such entertainment as was given to them.'

Fifteen children were executed; thirty-six were whipped every Sunday for a year before the church doors, and all the others were punished with varying degrees of severity.

Hunting for wild cats

Although in the Middle Ages domestic cats were loved, the wild cats living in forests were regarded as fair game. To hunt wild cats in the royal forests special licences were required. They were first issued in 1239 by Richard II to the Abbot of Peterborough.

Although the ladies in the convents were very fond of their domestic cats, they had nothing against wearing winter cloaks made of the skin of wild cats. In fact a law of 1127 prohibited the use of fur more expensive than that of wild cat by any abbess or nun.

Church cats

Most old churches used to keep cats to control mice. In Exeter Cathedral, there were specially made holes in the church doors which enabled the cats to freely enter the church. Bishop Cotton who was at Exeter from 1621 ordered his clergymen to make 'cat-holes' in every church. Money was put aside for the cathedral cats as their services were considered most valuable.

A Cornish clergyman, Reverend R S Walker, was a cat lover. He used to take all his nine cats into church. But the cats had to behave themselves in the sacred place. He excommunicated one of his favourite cats when it caught a mouse in the sanctuary.

Jewel protectors

When they are in a good mood, Siamese cats walk with tail erect. It curls slightly at the end like a finger. This habit of Siamese cats was made use of by the ladies of the Siamese court; they used to place their precious rings on the end of their cats' tails when bathing, in the belief that the cat would protect their valuable jewellery from thieves.

Feline bridge

In Tokyo there is a bridge dedicated to a cat that helped its poor and sick mistress by stealing small gold objects from a neighbouring money lender. The Nekomatabashi bridge is visited regularly by people who wish to honour the cat.

Mother of cats

The Prophet Mohammed was such a great lover of cats that he often used to hold his favourite cat in his arms while preaching to his followers. This cat was called Nuezza. One day Mohammed even cut the sleeve off his robe in order not to disturb the cat who was asleep on it.

After the prophet's death it became customary for many Muslims to take their own cats with them on the long pilgrimage to Mecca.

Wealthier pilgrims used special camels to carry their cats there. A woman attendant was usually appointed whose only duty was to care for the cats during the trip. She was popularly referred to as the 'Mother of Cats'.

Strange beliefs

France
The cat was the main object of festivities during harvest time at Briançon. Before scything began, a cat was decorated with ears of corn and ribbons laced with wildflowers. The cat was then carried in a procession to the cornfield. Whenever the reaper nicked himself with his scythe he would ask the ceremonial cat to lick his wound. When all the corn was harvested, the cat's decorations were removed and the animal was set free.

Holland

Some old Dutchmen still believe that people who dislike cats will be carried to the cemetery through rain. They also say that young people who care badly for their cats will have rain at their weddings.

Iran

In the past, people of Persia had the following advice for cat owners who wanted their pet to stay at home: measure the cat's tail with a piece of wood, cut the wood to size and burn it in the oven.

Ireland

The Irish used to claim that cats once had their own king and even parliament.

Italy

Ancient Romans considered the cat to be a household god. It had a special importance during such events as marriage or death. At marriages, the bride had to offer money for the cat as she entered her new home. At funerals, tributes also had to be paid to the cat to ensure protection in the afterlife.

Japan

Members of some Japanese sects claimed that a black patch on the back of a cat was a sacred mark. It was believed to signify that the cat was an abode of the soul of an ancestor.

When the Chinese introduced cats to Japan in the tenth century, they were so rare that only royal families were wealthy enough to own them. The cats were so precious in those days that it was believed that anyone who would kill a cat would be cursed, as well as his whole family. They would be haunted for the rest of their lives.

Madagascar
If you kick a cat it will start to steal chickens, say some inhabitants of the island. It is also believed in some regions that a pregnant cat must not be spoken of by its name.

Malaysia
The Jakurs venerate the cat. They believe that after they die a cat will lead them through hell to paradise. The cat will spray the infernal atmosphere with water, to reduce the temperature and make the journey more agreeable.

Burma
A religious order of North Burma had a temple which was called Lao-Tsun meaning 'abode of the gods'. In this temple they kept a hundred sacred cats. One of the cats called Sinh used to sit with a high priest at the foot of the statue of the goddess who presided over the transmutation of souls. The sacred cats were said to have the souls of human elders.

Russia
There was an old Russian belief that at the age of seven a black cat turns into a devil. Cat's brain was regarded as the most poisonous substance and it was an ingredient of the most powerful spells. The cat's tail was said to be an excellent cure for a number of ills.

It was believed that cat's tail has the power to bring good fortune.

It was customary to put a cat into a new cradle before a baby was born to drive away evil spirits.

Scandinavia
Freya was the Nordic goddess of love and fertility. She was depicted riding a chariot drawn by two grey cats. To secure good crops, farmers used to leave offerings of milk in the field for Freya's cats.

Freya was also the goddess of lovers and therefore Friday or Freya's Day was thought to be the best day for weddings. To please the goddess a cat had always to be present at a wedding ceremony.

Scotland
There was a belief in the old days that if a tomcat ejaculates when jumping over food any woman who ate the food would give birth to kittens. So strong was this belief that in 1654 a woman begged for an abortion because she believed she had kittens in her womb.

Tibet
Tibetans believe that if someone kills a cat — either accidentally or on purpose — the sins of the cat will be transferred to him; not only the sins of that cat but even the sins of the man who was incarnated in the cat.

Vatican
In 1484, Pope Innocent VIII declared that when witches go to the stake their cats must be burned with them. As late as the 1600s, just to own a cat might sometimes be sufficient evidence for a woman to be considered a witch.

West Africa
In parts of West Africa some people still believe that a lunar eclipse is caused by a cat eating the moon, but that the cat will release the moon if a special hand-clapping ritual is performed.

Chapter Nineteen

Cats in wars

Greatest feline hero of Stalingrad

Only one cat ever made it to the front page of the London *Times*. That was the female cat, Mourka. Her story was published on 13 January 1943 during World War II.

She lived in Stalingrad. She proved to be of great value to the Russian defenders during the long-lasting siege of the city. Mourka carried dispatches about gun emplacements through the constantly bombed suburbs of the city, through shelling that a human messenger would never survive.

German soldiers did not even suspect that a miserable looking cat could be of any harm.

For months, the clever cat fulfilled her dangerous mission and it was said that she never made a mistake. This unique cat's assistance was of tremendous military value to the Russians.

Cat suicide missions

In 1980, it became known that the CIA had trained cats to carry bombs. The information was contained in a document released to the American public under the US Freedom of Information Act.

Cats in service of the Pentagon

In 1968 Pentagon officials decided that cats would be perfect guides on raids in the night-time jungles of Vietnam. Results of trials were not those expected by the Pentagon strategists.

The first group of cats went on strike at the first sign of tropical rain. Other cats found more amusing pastimes. They began to play with the dangling pack-straps of the marching soldiers, forgetting their jobs completely. Even the cats that seemed willing often led their troops racing through thick bush in pursuit of field mice.

The operation cost thousands of dollars and was a complete failure. The Pentagon strategists had forgotten about the feline personality.

Cats winning wars

In the year 500 BC, the Persians attacked Pelusium (near Port Said in modern day Egypt). Despite clever tactics they were unable to conquer the Egyptians. It seemed the Persians would never win.

One day, though, their commander Cambyses ordered his soldiers to seize as many cats as they could find. He gave them eight days. In that time, a great number of cats were gathered. When the Egyptians next attacked, they saw an incredible number of cats running ahead of the Persian army. As well, each Persian soldier held a living cat in his arms. Cats were divinities in Egypt, and the soldiers refused to attack the Persians. To avoid killing the cats they surrendered without a fight.

This is not the only time cats were crucial to the outcome of a battle. During the World War II in Burma the Allied forces badly needed the help of locals to construct strategic roads. But the Burmese were unwilling to help. Japanese propaganda had persuaded them not to give any assistance to the Allies.

A British colonel who had excellent knowledge of local customs ordered his soldiers to collect as many white cats as they could. Soon he also had the silhouettes of white cats stencilled on army vehicles, giving the impression that cats were the emblem of the British army. Soldiers were also seen with live cats. The colonel knew that white cats were a symbol of good luck and beauty to the Burmese. When the Burmese saw so many white cats with the British they quickly changed sides and started to help the Allies.

Chapter Twenty

Great feline travellers

Incredible cat hitch-hiker

In September 1983 an eight-year-old black cat from Yarmouth, Norfolk hid herself under the bonnet of a car owned by Mr Fraser Robertson. Fraser Robertson discovered the cat, six hours later, after he travelled around 500 km towards Aberdeen in Scotland. The cat, covered in grime, was sitting behind the battery. Mr Robertson later pondered: 'How she survived six hours of non-stop driving I will never know. The engine was incredibly hot, and what with the petrol fumes, oil smoke and the noise, it must have been a terrifying experience for her.'

Mr Robertson fed the cat at a service station cafeteria and continued his journey. This time the hitch-hiking pussy travelled on the back seat.

Greatest feline train traveller

Toby loved to travel by train. While he was still a small kitten his resting place was the refreshment room at Carlisle Station, near the England–Scotland border. Soon, the handsome black cat became fascinated by rail travel. He became a well-known traveller when he was still very young.

Toby was such a common sight on London Midland and Scottish line that guards provided him with a tag with the inscription: 'If found please return to Carlisle Station'.

Toby clearly liked to travel into Scotland. He always boarded trains going north of Carlisle. Without exception he ignored south-bound trains. He preferred fish trains but also boarded those with a milk van.

Toby's longest trip was 245 miles to Aberdeen, and once he arrived at the ferry port of Stranraer, but refused to change the mode of transport to reach Ireland. The station master of Carlisle started to record Toby's rail trips but gave up when his journeys passed fifty.

Sadly Toby lost his life as a result of his unusual passion for trains. One day while he was walking across the tracks at Carlisle Station he failed to see an approaching train, and was hit.

Feline stowaway to Australia

Even animals seem to want to settle in the paradise down under that is Australia. However it's more difficult for a cat to sneak in unnoticed.

One British cat in 1990 found a solution to the seemingly impossible task. He hid inside a Mercedes Benz he found at a freight company in Kent. The car was bound for Port Adelaide, South Australia. The shippers sealed the container with the car inside, unaware of the cat's presence. The container might have been the cat's sea-going tomb, but fifty days later in Port Adelaide, customs officials discovered the emaciated cat still alive. Somehow he survived fifty days without food or drink. He was held for nine months in quarantine. He was then allowed to stay in the new country and was adopted by the owner of the car.

Travelled airline pussynger

Hamlet is a real champion traveller among cats. He flew twenty-five times around the world without leaving the plane. Hamlet got out of his cage while on a flight from Canada to London in a British Airways Jumbo jet. Despite a thorough search, he could not be found so the plane's staff eventually gave up.

But Hamlet had sneaked behind panelling in the hold. He landed in Jamaica, Kuwait and Australia. The plane landed twenty-five times in London alone, but the cat was not discovered. He was eventually found after six weeks of almost non-stop flying during a routine maintenance check at London airport. He is said to have survived on condensation.

Cat and kittens' epic journey

One hot summer, a Manhattan family left their apartment (taking their cat) to spend the vacation in the country. They rented a house about 160 km from Manhattan.

During their stay, the cat became pregnant and when it was time to return home she suddenly disappeared. The cat gave birth in a secret spot.

Eager to rejoin the family, the cat two months later travelled back home with one kitten in her mouth. To reach her destination the intrepid mother cat travelled with her baby a hundred miles through fields, towns and the busy streets of the city.

Soon the cat disappeared again. She returned two weeks later with another kitten in her mouth. This time, though the family decided to help. They put their amazing cat in the car and went back to the summer house and collected the remaining kittens.

Chapter Twenty-One

Cat friendships with other creatures

Cat-elephant friendship

Mark Twain tells the story of a cat in the zoo at Marseilles who was fond of an African elephant. The cat developed the habit of climbing up the elephant's hind leg to reach his huge back. He used to spend half the afternoon sleeping in the sun on top of the elephant.

At first the elephant used his trunk to put the cat down whenever it climbed up his body. But the stubborn cat did not easily give in, it simply climbed on again and again. Finally the elephant surrendered and let the cat climb whenever he liked. Eventually a great friendship developed between the two.

Cat mother and mouse baby

The motherhood instinct is so strong in cats that females readily become foster-mothers to other animals. The most unusual stories about feline foster mothers naturally concern fostering baby mice.

Early this century a cat living on a farm in Surrey had two kittens which were born and lived in a manger. Above the manger there was a mouse hole and a baby mouse lived there. The cat seemed not to be happy with only two babies so she decided to adopt the baby mouse. Believe it or not, the cat allowed the baby mouse to feed from her like her own feline babies.

The cat was so strongly attached to the baby mouse that each time the tiny mouse ran back into its hole, the cat cried after it and looked most unhappy until the baby mouse returned.

But the cat's attitude towards other mice was quite normal. When she discovered another mouse under the manger, she would quickly kill and eat it.

A cat in Oslo was said to have reared a whole litter of mice. A third fascinating case comes from England. There, a cat called Billie when he caught a mouse never killed it as most cats do. He took the captured mouse to the kitchen alive and invited it to eat his own food. While the mouse was eating dinner, the cat observed the scene with evident pleasure.

Cat mother and puppies

One day a Bedlington terrier in Marlborough (UK) had such a large litter of puppies that she was unable to care for all of them. The dog's owner took some of the puppies and handed them over to his cat who just had kittens of her own. The mother cat's response was very friendly and she cared for them as well as for her own kittens. She did not even allow people to touch the puppies.

Cat-dog language

W. H. Hudson wrote about a very small female cat who from early childhood lived with a dog. The two were close friends. When the cat gave birth to kittens, she found them very heavy and difficult to carry in her mouth. One day, she wanted to move them to a new place.

The cat showed the dog the new place she was making for the kittens and eventually the dog got the message; he picked up and carried each kitten in his mouth to the new nest place.

Feline savers of dogs

In October 1990 a poodle was attacked by a pit bull which somehow entered the yard where the poodle lived. The poodle's close friend, a cat who lived in the same house, immediately leaped from the roof of a nearby porch and landed, scratching, on the head of the pit bull. The cat saved the poodle's life.

In 1987 a cat saved collie puppies from a muskrat which attacked them.

The collie bitch was very weak from having given birth and she was unable to protect her newly born offspring. The family cat came to her defence. The cat slashed across the predator's unprotected nose and then got the muskrat behind its neck, shook it several times and tossed it out of the yard.

Kitten's friendship with a marmoset

Arthur Read was in charge of the Salmon Lane Lock of the Grand Union Canal. He owned a kitten and a marmoset. Both animals became friends and enjoyed playing together. When not playing they used to lie down together and gaze into the fire or sleep in each other's company. Sometimes the two friends climbed a rope in order to enter a big wire cage which hung on the wall. The marmoset would also embrace the kitten with his arms to protect it.

Feline-canary friendship

U.S. President Calvin Coolidge (1872-1933) had a pet canary. One day, Washington newspaperman Bascom Timmols came to the White House to interview the President accompanied by his cat. The cat and canary loved each other on sight. Eventually, President Coolidge sent the canary to the newspaperman's house to live with his cat friend. The canary used to walk up and down on the back of the cat and rest between his paws. The cat immensely enjoyed the singing of his little yellow friend.

Cat-zoo animals friendships

Incredible friendships of domestic cats with wild animals have been observed at the zoo in Wroclaw in the south-west of Poland. A few homeless cats roam in the zoo and the friends they have found there are truly unexpected. One cat began regularly visiting a snow leopard. Soon they began to eat and sleep together. One day, however, a girlfriend was brought for the pleasure of the snow leopard and the cat was forcibly removed from the cage. The cat did not give up easily, and for days he sat beside the cage staring at his powerful friend.

Another cat appeared at the baboon enclosure. The baboons readily accepted their new pal and refused to allow the cat to be taken away from them.

Another cat found its home in the cage of a wolf bitch. He used to eat with her and even sleep on her back. There were never any conflicts between the two and whenever the cat was late back from a walk the wolf howled. The cat always reacted immediately to the loud howling and quickly ran back to his friend. This friendship lasted several years until the wolf's death.

Chapter Twenty-Two

Cats with nine lives

Tough Macedonian cat

In 1974 a cat in Skopje, Macedonia, survived 53 hours entombed in a concrete wall. The cat, a pet of men working on a new building, vanished at exactly the time they were setting up planks to frame a concrete wall. When the timber was removed days later, the surprised labourers found their cat jammed between the bottom plank and the cement. The cat had survived by breathing through a small crack in the wood.

Cat under water

Three-year-old Peter the cat survived eight days underwater in the cabin of Dutch MV *Tjoba*, when it capsized and sank in the Rhine in 1964. Peter survived by keeping his head in an airpocket although the rest of his body was fully submerged. He was found and rescued when the ship was raised.

Tough pussies

Cats have demonstrated their ability to survive falls from improbable heights. Record holder in this endeavour appears to be Patricia a pregnant one-year-old cat. Her barbarous owners tried to get rid of their pet by throwing her from St John's Bridge in Portland, Oregon. Poor Patricia was thrown nearly 70 metres into the freezing Willamette River. She survived the fall and was pulled out by local fishermen who were surprised to find her alive. She was adopted by one of her rescuers. But she lost her kittens as a result of the fall.

Falling from tall buildings is a common mishap for cats. It has been calculated that in a single year in New York City some 85,000 cats fall from skyscrapers, and are treated by vets. Surprisingly, many survive.

Among them was a cat called Walter who fell eighteen floors in 1984.

His owner David Corr opened a window while cleaning his apartment. Walter jumped on to the window sill and fell, after losing his balance. David rushed downstairs without much hope of finding his pet alive but the cat landed in bushes and was in a reasonably good shape. David honoured his cat's remarkable rescue by renaming him Chuck Yeager, after the famous test pilot in the film, *The Right Stuff*. To commemorate the event David Corr ordered a cup for his pet with the following inscription: 'World High Altitude Freefall Drop'.

Cat demolition

The greatest cat saboteur in the world was probably a feline by the name of Sedgewick, a native of Cambridgeshire. In 1982, he nudged a 30,000 volt switch in a sub-station and cut off power to 40,000 local homes. When Sedgewick somehow managed to reach home some 30 metres from the sub-station, according to his owner he looked 'like a burnt tyre'. With the help of the local vet he fully recovered from his mishap.

Cats 100; dogs zero

In 1870, a building in Paris called Halle au Bles, was so infested with rats that it was thought necessary to enlist an army of cats to destroy them. The rats were attacking grain sacks, but rat traps had proved ineffective.

The recruited cats did a good job, but they themselves reproduced at such a rate that they became a menace themselves.

Six bull-dogs were then employed to drive the cats out of the building. The cats, however, simply sat in the rafters and the dogs could do nothing. Then it was decided to starve the cats to death. That plan, did not work either, because some old ladies in the area became involved in clandestine feeding of the 'poor' cats.

Then, poison was tried. It was thought it would destroy the cats in a matter of a few hours. But the cats knew the meat was poisonous and refused to touch it.

Instead, the unsuspecting dogs ate the meat and all died. The cats continued to be fed by the generous old ladies.

Chapter Twenty-Three

Cats who save people

Cat his sole means of support

In 1992 a Russian newspaper reported that an eighty-year-old man who lived in the town of Lubinsk claimed that he was only able to survive thanks to the very clever cat he owned.

Every day his cat caught a pigeon and brought it home; the old man made a soup with it, and this was his only source of food.

Realising the great importance of the cat for his survival, the old man attempted to insure his feline benefactor with the state insurance authorities. The insurance office refused, however, to grant the extraordinary wish. But he complained to president Boris Yeltsin, arguing that the insurance of his cat was essential since without the generous creature he would die of starvation.

Cat warning

Bogdan Zagorski's guests were truly perplexed. His cat Macius had been sitting on the sofa for more than two hours, motionless, its eyes fixed on the ceiling.

At first everybody ignored the cat while they played cards. Gradually, however, everybody realised that the cat's behaviour was weird.

Macius normally was a cat who either slept on the sofa or ran restlessly around the house trying to catch somebody's attention when he wanted to play or eat.

Now he looked like a stone monument of a terrified and deranged cat. 'Perhaps, your cat is mentally ill', said one of the guests, smiling ironically at the owner. Zagorski said nothing, furious at the suggestion. The other guests burst with laughter.

Suddenly Macius twitched. He eyed the card players with a grim look as if they were all stupid and raced to the door leading to the back yard. In no time he was outside. Minutes later the guests were terrified to hear the cat uttering an immensely loud pitiful wail.

The frightened guests and Zagorski rushed outside, convinced that something awful had happened. But the cat looked healthy enough and there were no dogs or other dangerous creatures in the backyard. Everything looked perfectly normal.

Only seconds later a rumbling noise was heard from the house, and the startled guests watched as a huge slab of the roof collapsed in the lounge room where they had been sitting moments before.

The cat had saved the lives of twelve people.

Belling a cat

Dora Zielinska made a firm decision. If her cat would not stop ringing the dinner bell that hung on a rope in the hall, she would kick the cat out of her home and never let it in again.

She would take the cat to the nearest animal refuge and state that she was unable to care for it. She was so annoyed by the constant unnecessary noise and the persistent complaints of neighbours that she was ready for even the most drastic solution to her problem.

Somehow, as if by clairvoyance, the cat understood, and for a whole week all was quiet.

Then a few days later, Mrs Zielinska fell from a ladder leading to the attic and broke her hip. She could not move and could not scream loud enough. She knew for the last seven days the cat had been an obedient pet who would not ring the bell.

But luckily the cat was not so dumb. He soon understood the gravity of her situation and began to ring the bell so vigorously that a furious neighbour burst in and then saw what had happened. Dora was given prompt medical help, and she decided never again to make decisions about her cat.

Cat saves child from drowning

In Sydney, a small boy was drowning in the backyard swimming pool while his mother was busy preparing lunch. The family pet, a fat black cat, was sitting near the pool and saw what was happening.

She immediately realised she must act.

She began to howl, and although she was usually very quiet the child's mother did not at first take any notice of the cat's appeal. Soon though, the howling was so intense that the woman went outside to see what was going on. She arrived just in time to save her little boy.

Cat saves boy from vicious dog

One day Janek, a small Polish boy was returning home when a large German shepherd attacked him.

The dog clamped its jaws around the boy's right arm and began shaking him. There were no people around to help the boy.

But he was lucky. Help came from the most unexpected quarter. The boy's cat witnessed the attack, and knowing he could not confront the powerful dog, climbed the nearest tree. He then leaped from it straight on to the back of the dog. He sank his claws and teeth deep into the dog's flesh.

The German shepherd quickly released the boy and ran away terrified by the unexpected attack.

In this ingenious way the little cat was able to save his master's life.

Cat who hypnotised cobras

In 1922, in India a cat saved an army officer from the attack of a deadly cobra.

One day while walking on his verandah he saw the snake rearing up ready to strike.

Expecting every moment to feel its fangs, he wondered at the delay of the deadly stroke when, glancing behind him, he saw his cat crouching and gazing intently at the reptile with mesmeric effect.

The cobra seemed to have been hypnotised by the cat. It was unable to move for a while and the officer was able to kill it.

Feline snake charmer

When Varee Reeves of Mesa, Arizona, heard a strange hissing sound she thought her recently installed sprinkler system had broken down. But the hissing came from her new Turkish angora cat, who evidently was furious. Varee's two-year-old son was in the backyard so she thought he might be teasing the new pet. She decided to investigate. What she saw was shocking beyond imagination. A huge rattlesnake was moving slowly towards her son and blocking the snake's path was the tiny angora.

She was moving up and down, twisting and turning. It appeared as if the cat in the role of a snake charmer was trying to persuade the dangerous snake to concentrate its attention on her instead of the boy.

Varee immediately rang the police. Soon though, it became clear that the cat had the upper hand. The snake appeared to have become scared of the cat; it relaxed its coiled striking posture and began to retreat, gradually and cautiously edging away.

From time to time the snake stopped retreating, as if considering a new attack. Each time the brave cat stared down the snake as if trying to hypnotise the evil creature. Soon the defending cat got reinforcements. Two police officers and a man from the reptile control bureau arrived and the reptile handler caught the snake and dropped it into a sack.

Varee honoured her brave little cat by giving her a new name: 'Brave Woman'.

Chapter Twenty-Four

Funny feline stories

Pussy rhymester

Geoffry Handley-Taylor, the first editor of *Who's Who* was a lover of cats and something of a joker. He had a ginger tomcat who liked to sit on his desk observing his master at work. Handley-Taylor repaid his favourite cat's close attachment in a unique way.

He made the cat a great poet. He included Honey Grindle — his cat in the *International Who's Who in Poetry*. Naturally he did not tell anybody, except his close friend John Masefield, who also adored cats, that Mr Grindle was a cat.

The entry ran as follows: Grindle (Honey) (Fanny Beckett), born 21 April 1937. Publications: Roof Poems, Cat Fancier's Guide. Recreations: Bird watching, fishing. Clubs: Manx, Derby Bowl.

Neat puss

Samantha was a cat who worked hard daily to keep her neighbourhood tidy. Whenever she noticed someone throwing litter on the pavement or lawn she flashed in and picked up the discarded object. She was even seen following school children to pick up crisp packets they dropped.

One day, however, Samantha carried her zeal for neatness too far. She stole two $5 notes from a table in a neighbour's house. The cat committed the offence when she went through a bedroom window, gathered the notes and deposited them in the garden of her owner. Unfortunately, Samantha's master was a policeman.

Cat defeated by mouse

One day in Devon, Percy the cat refused to accept the sight of a mouse drinking his milk. He was just about to attack the mouse and get rid of it when the courageous mouse bit the cat, taking a slice out of his nose.

The cat's mistress was a generous and understanding lady, so she put down another saucer with milk, this time for the mouse.

Love for a cat has no bounds

Francois Desroches, from Poitiers, France, is among those whose love for his cat knew no limits. When the cat Timmy disappeared one day, Francois searched for him frantically although he was in poor health after a heart attack. Despite lack of success Francois did not give up. He closed his bakery and spent his life savings on a further search for his missing friend. He had printed 70,000 posters and sent them over a wide area.

Months passed, and it seemed that nobody had seen his cat. Francois was depressed by the disappearance of his feline friend and refused to reopen the bakery. Finally his business collapsed completely as other bakers opened in the town.

One night while conducting his regular search, Timmy leaped into his arms from the undergrowth. As Francois later commented 'He cost me a fortune, but he's worth it'.

Clever politician and cats

One day, Charles James Fox, the eighteenth-century statesman was walking with the Prince of Wales, who later became George IV. He greatly surprised the Prince by saying that he was sure that if they would each choose a side of the street to walk on he would always see more cats than the Prince. The future monarch was even more astounded when the statesman offered to lay a bet. The Prince promptly agreed, convinced that Fox was either out of his mind or a compulsive gambler.

The Prince could not believe his eyes when on the side chosen by the Fox, cats appeared one after another. Not a single cat was to be seen on the side where the Prince was walking. In fact, when they reached the end of the street, they both counted no fewer than thirteen cats all on the side Fox had chosen.

The Prince paid the bet, but convinced there must be some logical explanation. he asked the politician about how he won.

Fox eagerly answered his question: 'Your Royal Highness took, of course, the shady side of the way as the most agreeable. I knew that the sunny side would be left to me, and cats always prefer the sunshine.'

Cats more important than women

In Oklahoma (USA) cats are treated as more important than women by the local law.

Beating a woman can earn the offender 90 days behind bars. Kicking a cat is a crime that can result in a sentence of years in gaol.

A police officer slammed his girlfriend's head into a wall, pulled her by the hair and kicked her. His crime is punishable by up to 90 days in gaol. Another police officer became angry and kicked a cat at the airport. His sentence could be up to five years in gaol plus a fine of up to $5000.

The police officer who kicked the cat would be automatically discharged from the police force; the man who inflicted such harm on his girlfriend would not.

Loo fat cat

Tiddles was a famous toilet tomcat of London. He lived in the ladies' lavatory at Paddington station for thirteen years. He was one of the fattest cats in the nation and weighed over 14 kg.

Tiddles came to the city loo in 1970 when he was just a tiny six-week old kitten. He was warmly received by Mrs June Watson, the toilet attendant. She decided to adopt him. She cared for Tiddles and shared her lunch cheese with him.

Visiting ladies accepted the male presence in the busy loo and Tiddles, who grew into a handsome and big cat, lived there like a king. Every day the ladies who used the loo brought the pet the best treats. The women's generosity was so great that Mrs Watson found it difficult to accept all the gifts. Soon, to keep all the food, Tiddles was provided with a personal fridge.

Tiddles, the loo cat was so constantly fed and became so fat that few cats could compete with him in size. He became famous all over the world. Letters addressed to the celebrated cat in the London loo even started to arrive from overseas. June Watson was kept busy collecting all the press cuttings about her famous pet. The cuttings increased even further the fame of the cat.

In 1982, when Tiddles reached the weight of 13.6 kg, he became London's heaviest cat, and was named 'London Fat Cat Champion'.